Great Danes

Ch. Dolf v.d. Saalburg. Statue donated to the Kennel Club by the late Bill Siggers. (Photo: S. Ball, by kind permission of the Kennel Club.)

GREAT DANES

AN OWNER'S COMPANION
Karina Le Mare

The Crowood Press

First published in 1992 by
The Crowood Press Ltd
Ramsbury, Marlborough
Wiltshire SN8 2HR

This impression 1995

British Library Cataloging in Publication Data

A catalogue record for this book is available from
the British Library.

ISBN 1 85223 316 8

Dedication
Dedicated to my mother Dagmar Hielm Kirkefjord, whose
gentle hands taught me the love and care of animals, and my
son Noah Le Mare who has inherited this love and accepts the
hard work such love demands.

Throughout this book, 'he', 'him' and 'his' have been used as
neutral pronouns and therefore refer to both sexes.

Typeset by Taurus Graphics, Kidlington, Oxfordshire
Printed in Great Britain by Redwood Books, Trowbridge, Wiltshire

Contents

Acknowledgements

I should like to thank Eric and Joan Hutton of the famous Merrowlea prefix, who helped, advised and encouraged me. They also 'allowed' me to own Ch. Miss Freedom of Merrowlea who became my first Champion and greatest brood-bitch of all. I would also thank my ex-husband Gordon Le Mare for his help and encouragement at the out-set of my career in 1968, and Bill Siggers for the very first and very treasured Challenge Certificate.

I am indebted to David Wickins who has given me so many mem-ories, including those of his many Great Danes – all named Jason or Tina; to Mandy Toms for being a great handler; to Norman Blagrave, a great puppy rearer and dog lover; to Anna Molcanovs for years of ded-ication to the Helmlake Danes; to Wendy Harris, who came to Wey Farm at the tender age of seventeen and has been at my right hand ever since; and to Jacky Stanley, who has worked with me at Wey Farm since 1980.

I am very grateful to the many Dane people all over the world with whom I have forged firm friendships based on our mutual love of the breed; and to all those who supplied photographs from their collec-tions for use in this book, with special thanks to the Great Dane Club. I am also grateful to Tony Schanning Ling for all his help with statistics.

I also wish to thank the Rudolph Steiner School in Bergen, Norway, who taught respect and reverence for all living animals as a complete way of life, a philosophy that has made me what I am – a dreamer. Dr Albert Schweitzer was a great practitioner of this ideal, and the short time I spent in his company in Africa cemented this philosophy and set my path in life.

Finally, I should like to make a very special acknowledgement and public thank you to Adele Summers, partner in the famous Toydom prefix. Without her extensive work on the manuscript, and her knowl-edge and expertise, this book would never have come to fruition.

Introduction

Welcome to the world of the Great Dane, a world full of fascination, enjoyment, fulfilment and one that I have been associated with for many years. I hope that through this book I may be able to impart some of my ideas, experiences and general knowledge to you so that you in turn may learn to enjoy being a part of this magnificent breed.

In the following chapters I shall lead you through the breed's past, introducing many of its descendants, on to the actual care of your new puppy and the various aspects of rearing. In later chapters there will be information on showing and judging, and also how to train your dog either for the show ring or merely for your own satisfaction in having a well-behaved and easily manageable dog. There will be advice on breeding, nutrition and veterinary matters, and information to bring you up to date with some famous kennels of today – many up and coming ones – and also those of yesteryear.

1

The History of the Breed

It may seem hard to imagine that the dog lying quietly at your feet is the product of a fascinating and highly complex ancestry. The Great Danes that you see today either in the show ring or in the street differ from the ones of yesteryear. A dog resembling a Dane can be seen in many carvings and pictures dating back as far as two thousand years ago. Most of these seemed to belong to tribes in Asia, predominantly to the Assyrians in the western part of the continent. These tribes were great traders, sellers and bargainers of wares, and one can almost visualize their caravans heading over the vast empty expanses ready to do business with the various cultures, including those of ancient Greece and the Roman Empire.

Their goods would include beautiful cloths and treasures including silver and highly prized ivory. Deals would be struck and a certain amount of bartering no doubt went on. Other items and commodities would therefore be included, some of which it is thought were the Assyrians' dogs. It is believed that this link is tenable owing to a similar type of large hunting dog being recorded amongst the Romans, Greeks and Assyrians. As with many of today's breeds, the Great Dane's 'roots' are more than a little hazy, for dogs resembling the Dane have been recorded in many parts of Europe, as far east as Russia and as far south as Tibet and India.

When the Romans ruled part of Great Britain, they not only took captives to send to Rome as slaves, but rounded up many of the island race's dogs for transportation to Rome. This 'trade' became such an important issue that in Winchester, which became known as the 'City of Dogs', a procurer from Rome was installed to ensure that suitable animals were found for this purpose. He was grandly known as the Procurator Cynogie.

The dogs of that time were thought to have been a hunting type of animal, resembling a mastiff, and it is most probable that they were returned to Rome to interbreed with the native dogs there. No doubt it was done to improve the quality, and it is thought that they were probably bred for fighting, or indeed hunting. The British dogs were reported to have been very strong with wide jaws and would probably have complemented the lighter and sleeker hunting dogs of the Romans. Together with the mastiff-type dogs that were rounded up, it is also thought that deerhounds were included in these shipments to the nucleus of the Empire.

Prior to this, the Romans probably bred from dogs of Northern India and Tibet and from Molossia in the northern part of Greece. It is believed that the dog that began to emerge at that time in Rome was a result of these various types: the Tibetan, the Molossian and the mastiff.

Whereas in Rome these Dane-like dogs had been bred to fight each other, in the Middle Ages boar hunting was very popular in Europe amongst the upper echelons of society. Dogs were therefore bred to be able to chase, corner and attack this quarry. These dogs, known as Alaunts, were split into two particular types. One was a hunting Alaunt, which was highly prized for having a terrific scent for its prey, and the other was a less valuable Alaunt used to pin down the quarry that their opposite number had already tracked down. These dogs, it is thought, were mainly found in Germany, having been brought to that country by a group known as Alans who had settled there.

Although the dogs of this era did not closely resemble the Great Dane of today, there appears to be a connection and a certain likeness to the present-day dog. Many of the boarhounds in England had been cultivated by crossing a mastiff type with a greyhound type (one presumes this gave substance and strength to height and elegance). These in turn were bred with some of the European hunting dogs, notably those of France and Spain.

Probably one of the closest links to the Dane of today from yester-year was a mastiff style of dog that originated in England at Lyme Park around the 1500s, known as a Lyme Mastiff. These dogs were highly popular throughout England and the rest of Europe amongst the courts of the aristocracy. The height of their popularity is recorded as being between 1500 and 1700, and it is generally felt that the Lyme Mastiff had a very important part to play in the development of the breed as we know it today.

The thrill of boar hunting at that time increased, resulting in vast packs and quite incredible records being set up. One such record was set in 1563 when a nobleman named Landgraf Philipp was responsible with his hounds for the demise of 2,572 wild boar. As time went on, the English type of mastiff, known as the 'English Dogge', decreased in popularity and by the 1700s they were no longer favoured as a suitable cross with their European counterparts, notably the German stock. It appears that at this time the Germans became increasingly in favour of developing their own bloodlines, declining to import any more dogs from England.

The pick of the newly styled German dogs became highly desirable. They were bred for size, and the largest and most sought after were the Kammerhunde or Chamber Dogs. These were set apart from the others by being given gilded collars. Next to these came the Leibhunde or Life Dogs, which had a silver finish to their collars. With the introduction of the names Kammerhunde and Leibhunde, other names were bestowed, such as Fanghund (which was eventually replaced by the name Hatzrude), Boarhund, Saupacker, and Saufanger (translated, it means 'dog used for hunting wild boars'). These titles described the work or ability of that particular type of dog.

From the Middle Ages right through to the eighteenth and nineteenth centuries, the Great Dane gradually evolved, eventually to emerge at the first show to be held in Germany. This show took place in Hamburg in 1863. Eight 'Danish Doggen' and seven 'Ulmer Doggen' were recorded as being shown. From the descriptions received from that day one could speculate quite easily that they were what are now known as the Great Dane. In fact, one of the adjectives given to describe them was 'grave looking', an apt description of the breed we know today. It is rumoured that two of these dogs were purchased from the show by none other than the Tsar of Russia.

By 1869 both variations, Danish and Ulmer, had increased in popularity in Germany. In this particular year the entry recorded for the Danish Doggen at the Hamburg-Altona show was fifteen while the Ulmer Doggen numbered twelve. Seven years later once again an increase is noted, the entries being twenty-four and forty-five respectively. The interesting point at this stage is that for some reason the Danish Doggen had papers stating them to be natives of Denmark, but it is known that not one of these dogs had had any actual physical connection with Denmark, having all been born and bred in Germany.

In 1876 an important stage in the history of the breed was reached when it was decided that it was virtually impossible to carry on with the breed segregated into Danish and Ulmer and it was proposed that they be officially 'christened' the Deutsche Dogge. With this decision it was thought that the confusion had been settled and that this would be the name forever more. However, this was not to be. There cannot be many breeds to have suffered so many altercations over their 'title'. In

1879 the name was altered once again. It was decided that the heavier-built dogs would go under the name of Danish Dogs while the lighter dogs became Ulmer Doggen. The whole process had turned almost full circle. Although these names had now been decided upon, it was also decided that brindle-coloured dogs should go under the name of Hatzruden (literally translated it means 'Wolf Dog'). To cause further confusion, fawns and occasionally blues were placed for some indescribable reason in the category of Danish Dogs whether they were light or heavy.

The harlequins, which had now become recognized and were very well favoured, were known as Tiger Dogs. One would have thought that this title would have been accorded to the brindles. In fact, the harlequin was put into this category for its resemblance to the Tiger Horse, which resembles what we would now call a piebald, that is, white with black patches. The harlequins first found popularity predominantly in the southernmost part of Germany, but as time progressed they were 'discovered' by owners in the north of the country and consequently became highly sought after. In fact, as time went on, they became numerically stronger in that area. By the year 1880 the confusion over these different labels had proved too much even for the stoutest fancier; steps were taken to ensure that the differences in the names were sorted out and the Dane emerged officially under the banner of Deutsche Dogge.

By this time in Germany many kennels had become established whose aim was to promote the native Deutsche Dogge. Max Hartenstein had acquired his first dog in 1874, a Wurttembergischer Hatzrude who was named Bosco. Two years later he purchased another, named Bella. This pair provided his initial success with the Deutsche Dogge and cemented the course of breed history. Another early pioneer was Mr Mebter, who had considerable success in the show ring after he started in the breed in 1878.

Mr B. Ulrich was another notable breeder of the day, his male line exerting a strong influence on the breed in Germany through such dogs as Harras II, Cerini and Hannibal I, this last dog regarded as most probably one of the best specimens of the time. Hannibal was purchased by Mr Ulrich for the astounding sum of one hundred and fifty pounds, something of a small fortune in those days. A certain mystery surrounds this reportedly superb dog for not a lot is known of his ancestry.

There are also two schools of thought as to what eventually happened to him. He was sold to England by Mr Ulrich, that part of his life we know for a fact, but there the mystery begins. One report is that he left England after being sold to Russia, another is that he was found dead in his kennel, having strangled himself.

The Schwalbennest kennel in Berlin favoured the blues. This line was known for many fine dogs and bitches, in particular the bitch Vesta.

The breed continued to grow in popularity in the 1880s until in 1887 at a show at Stuttgart a staggering entry of three hundred Great Danes was recorded. The year 1888 saw the foundation of the Deutscher Doggenclub, which was unique in being a club formed for one particular breed. Another interesting point is that, considering the growth and popularity of the breed in Germany while it was suffering its ups and downs in Great Britain, the English Great Dane Club was formed five years prior to its German cousin. One year later, the Kennel Club in England recognized the breed officially. With the foundation of the Deutscher Doggenclub the entries recorded throughout the twilight years of the nineteenth century averaged at one hundred plus. Fascination for the breed was steadily increasing and it is thought that in the year 1892 the first official Breed Standard was drawn up.

While it was gaining strength and popularity in its homeland, the Great Dane or Deutsche Dogge began to find friends in other parts of the globe and many dogs left nineteenth-century Germany for other shores, primarily for England (a reversal of the previous policy of importing dogs), other parts of Europe, notably France and Holland, and over the Atlantic to the United States.

Great Danes have been associated with the famous, including notables such as Alexander Pope the great eighteenth-century English poet, and the German chancellor Prince Otto von Bismarck. Wonderful stories are known of these two characters and their faithful dogs. Alexander Pope was subject to sudden changes of mood, much of which no doubt was owed to the fact that his health was poor. These varying shifts of mood made him almost manic and his friendships with people were, at the most, short-lived. All his shortcomings, though, were forgiven by his most devoted companion, his faithful Bounce. For, as we all know, our four-legged companions think no worse of us for all our indiscretions or any weaknesses we may have. Not only was Bounce his constant companion, he was also his saviour.

One dark night after Pope was carried to his bed by a recently employed valet, he was awakened from his slumber to see the figure of a man standing over him with a knife. Fear and panic struck at the poet and he screamed for help and assistance. No one in the immediate vicinity heard his pleas, only Bounce. Alerted by his master's cries, he leapt across the room at the would-be murderer and brought him to the floor. The assailant in fact turned out to be the valet who only a few hours earlier had carried his employer to his bed-chamber, and for some inexplicable reason returned to harm him. The uncanny thing about the whole business was that Bounce had taken an immediate dislike to this new servant at the start of his employment. Did he sense something in the man's character, you may ask? We shall never know. What we do know is that the more you live and learn about Danes, the more you realize how intelligent and knowing they are!

Prince Otto von Bismark was a devotee of this breed. His association with the Dane is legendary. One of his particular favourites was Tyras who was always at his master's side. On one occasion Bismarck was involved in a heated conversation with the Russian Prime Minister of the time. As the conversation became more intense Tyras suddenly took complete exception to the excessive waving of the Russian's arms and promptly leapt upon the visiting head of state, rendering them both in an unceremonious heap on the floor. So well known was Tyras and his association with the German chancellor and so revered by his master that on the occasion of the dog's death an announcement was made by cable to all four corners of the earth. The Prince's links with the breed spanned almost his whole life, and one of his Danes was a present to him from Kaiser Wilhelm himself.

Returning to the evolvement of the Great Dane. During the pursuit of wild boars many dogs were hurt, maimed or, in extreme cases, mortally wounded. Their ears were one of the most vulnerable parts of their bodies. To a cornered, frantic and dangerous boar these were easy prey and it was a common occurrence for a dog to have his ears mangled, torn and shredded. Because of this it became the practice to remove the ear flaps of the dog completely, or to crop them. Often the ear flaps were totally cut away, but as times changed this practice changed and one would assume that in order to enhance the look of the dog a new fashion was set in that the ears were then cropped, to result eventually in the look that is still favoured in parts of Europe and in the USA today.

Up until the end of the nineteenth century it was also common practice to do this in the United Kingdom, until the then Prince of Wales (the future King Edward VII) uttered his disapproval of this cosmetic surgery. When steps were taken to change this practice, this caused great consternation amongst the fancy, but by 27 February 1895 a rule was passed by the Kennel Club forbidding the cropping of Great Danes in Britain. After 1901 it was decreed that no dogs with cropped ears could be shown in this country. This hard and fast rule issued by the Kennel Club (in fact, it has never been classed as an illegal practice) resulted in many breeders of the time discontinuing their involvement with the breed.

It was around this time that the breed in the UK had been taking an upward path in popularity but as a result of this edict this trend was reversed. Coincidentally, at this point there was also a rabies scare sweeping the country. Unfortunately, at that period of the breed's history, temperament was causing a certain amount of concern; they were not quite the amiable or trusting dog that we know today. One of the results of the rabies scare was that restrictions were imposed calling for dogs to be muzzled and restrained. Many of the dogs became extremely unhappy and as a result a vast majority of them ended up being destroyed.

Thus the breed was travelling along a very difficult and rocky path. Another method of preventing rabies from running rife here was the introduction of a period of quarantine which immediately greatly reduced the number of German-bred dogs entering these shores, and this impediment further disrupted the fancy in the UK.

Shortly after the inception of The Great Dane Club in 1883, came their first show in 1885. With the breed at this time in the ascendency, an entry of sixty dogs was recorded. One of the founders of this club was a gentleman named Mr Adcock whose support, enthusiasm and patronage was partly responsible for the club's formation. One of his dogs was aptly named Satan, for he is reported to have possessed such an evil temper that he accosted a Newfoundland one day and, had he not been restrained, would have killed it. He is believed to have been a large heavy dog, weighing in at approximately 150lbs (68kg). He was dark in colour and had a type of head and jaw that was stronger than those favoured today. However, Mr Adcock was an avid lover of the breed and, apart from the terrible Satan who was obviously quite a handful, he was the owner of another dog, Ivanhoe, a consistent winner at the shows of those days.

The Great Dane had now been fully integrated into dogdom, so much so that a Standard was drawn up nine years prior to its German counterpart. It is thought that, as both sets of Standards hardly differ at all, they were probably based on an early description given by a gentleman named Herr Scheimeideberg, which read as follows:

Victor of Redgrave (1897). (Reproduced by kind permission of the Great Dane Club.)

Figure high, elegant, head rather long; nose of medium length, thick not pointed – point of nose large, black, except with Tiger dogs, where the same may be flesh coloured or spotted; lip trifle over-hanging, ears placed high and pointed, eyes brown, not too light (except with Tiger dogs which often have glassy eyes); earnest and sharp look, neck pretty long and strong; without dewlap; chest broad and deep; back long and straight; toes closed, nails strong and long; thigh bone muscular; knees deep, almost like a Greyhound; tail not too long; hardly to reach the hocks and to be carried in a straight line with the back, never to be curly; the coat of the whole body, and particularly the tail, to be short and smooth; back dew claws are allowed on the hind feet if they are firm not loose; colour bright black, wavy, yellow, blue, if possible without any marks, or if striped usually with glassy eyes.

The original English Standard that was drawn up made little of colour; this was particularly noticeable as harlequins were not even referred to.

Having gone through the various transitions of the breed, we are now at the point where the cropping regulations had changed the structure of the breed in the UK. With the disappearance of many of the breed's earliest enthusiasts, it was eventually decided by a handful of stalwart breeders to hold a meeting at Crufts one year. There it was proposed that the club be reformed and Mr Hood Wright, who had initiated the meeting, was made Honorary Secretary. The President was Mr Leadbetter who had enjoyed great success with his kennel, especially with a harlequin named Czar who was imported from Europe in 1897 after having had considerable success over there. Another of his dogs, Ch. Count Fritz, was born in Germany and as his parents were top-winning Continental show dogs, he would have been a great attraction.

With the migration of Great Danes from Germany to various shores, it was not long before they were finding favour in America. The first Dane recorded in the USA was owned by a Francis Butler of New York and was called Prince; he probably originated from Germany. Another Dane worth mentioning here, who is also believed to be from German stock, was called Imperator. This dog resided in Chicago where he was placed at stud for the princely sum of twenty guineas and was described as being 'the largest dog in the world'.

With their increasing popularity in their new homeland, classes were eventually put on for them in 1890, the initial entry being thirty-four dogs. I have already referred to some of the Danes of this time possessing rather aggressive temperaments, and the same pattern seemed to follow in America. In fact, this temperament factor caused such trouble that a Mr Lincoln who was a show superintendent at the New York Show attempted to have the breed banned. It seems hard to imagine that these are the same loving dogs that grace our homes and our lives today.

Mrs Hatfield with a team of her famous harlequin Great Danes.
(Reproduced by kind permission of the Great Dane Club.)

By 1889 enthusiasm for Great Danes in the USA was so strong that their first breed club was formed, the American Speciality Club, now called The Great Dane Club of America. By the year 1890 the number of American Champions made up totalled fourteen, with brindles being the numerically stronger, eleven in fact. The remaining three included two harlequins and one fawn. Obviously, time and understanding had ironed out those initial trials and tribulations, for in 1905 the Great Dane was riding on the crest of a wave in America and was reported as having a higher percentage of good specimens than any other breed.

With the advent of the twentieth century, the breeding of Great Danes gathered momentum back in the UK. One of the great kennels at this time was the Redgraves, belonging to Violet Horsfall. It is felt that the work and devotion she put into her breeding programme had a great bearing on the breed in this country. Her lines were founded on Germanic bloodlines including the great Nero. It is felt that she was the pathfinder of the modern Dane in Britain, her bloodlines being behind many of the fawns and brindles seen in the ring today. She bred and owned such dogs as Ch. Viola, Ch. Therr, Ch. Viceroy and Ch. Hannibal of Redgrave.

An incident occurred then that sent tremors of excitement around the ringside of yesterday when a showdown happened between Ch. Hannibal and the highly rated Ch. Bosco Colonia. The German dog had been brought over to compete against the cream of stock here. It appears that his owner, Herr Dobleman, felt quite confident his dog would emerge victorious. I imagine that you could have heard a pin drop when it came down to the final decision, and Ch. Hannibal was put above the German challenger.

After all the years of breeding and showing it is interesting to note that Violet Horsfall retired from the breed at the pinnacle of her success. Another English kennel, a contemporary of the Redgraves and sharing equal success, was the Stapletons, owned by Mrs Spark. One of her most famous Danes was a harlequin known as Superba of Stapleton.

The Great Dane had entered the twentieth century as a well-established and popular breed especially in Germany, the USA and – after all the aforementioned trials and tribulations – the United Kingdom. The breeding lines and programmes in these countries were well set on course for the enhancement of the breed. However, because of the intensity of war between 1914 and 1918, the breeding of the Deutsche Dogge was practically wiped out, with its English cousin being severely restricted as the carnage swept on and on.

With breeding at a virtual standstill in the native land of the Deutsche Dogge, many beautiful dogs died as a result of privation and lack of food as the war progressed. Many were used to help pull trucks on the field of battle in an effort to keep the various supplies and services operable. But although these animals almost became extinct, interest in the Deutsche Dogge never wavered. From the armistice in 1918 up until the Second World War, the torch was picked up and rekindled by fanciers and breeders devoted to restoring and encouraging the breed as we know it today.

2

The Breed Standard

There are three official Breed Standards for our breed: the German Standard, the American Standard and the UK Standard. The Breed Standard is the set guide-lines by which a Great Dane is assessed, judged or bred for.

The UK Breed Standard

(Reproduced by kind permission of the Kennel Club of Great Britain)

General Appearance.

Very muscular, strongly though elegantly built, with look of dash and daring, of being ready to go anywhere and do anything. Head and neck carried high, tail in line with back, or slightly upwards, but never curled over hindquarters. Elegance of outline and grace of form most essential.

Characteristics

Alert expression, powerful, majestic action displaying dignity.

Temperament

Kindly without nervousness, friendly and outgoing.

Head and Skull

Head, taken altogether, gives idea of great length and strength of jaw. Muzzle or foreface broad, skull proportionately narrow, so that whole head when viewed from above and in front, has appearance of equal breadth throughout. Length of head in proportion to height of dog. Length from nose to point between eyes about equal or preferably of greater length than from this point to back of occiput. Skull flat, slight indentation running up centre, occipital peak not prominent. Decided rise or brow over the eyes but not abrupt stop between them; face well chiselled, well filled in below eyes with no appearance of being pinched: foreface long, of equal depth throughout. Cheeks showing as little lumpiness as possible, compatible with strength. Underline of head, viewed in profile, runs almost in a straight line from corner of lip to corner of jawbone, allowing for fold of lip, but with no loose skin hanging down. Bridge of nose very wide, with slight ridge where cartilage joins bone (this is a characteristic of breed). Nostrils large, wide and open, giving blunt look to nose. Lips hang squarely in front, forming right angle with upper line of foreface.

Eyes

Fairly deep set, not giving the appearance of being round, of medium size and preferably dark. Wall or odd eyes permissible in harlequins.

Ears

Triangular, medium size, set high on skull and folded forward, not pendulous.

Mouth

Teeth level. Jaws strong with a perfect, regular and complete scissor bite, i.e. the upper teeth closely overlapping the lower teeth and set square to the jaws.

Neck

Neck long, well arched, quite clean and free from loose skin, held well up, well set in shoulders, junction of head and neck well defined.

Forequarters

Shoulders muscular, not loaded, well sloped back, with elbows well under body. Forelegs perfectly straight with big flat bone.

Body

Very deep, brisket reaching elbow, ribs well sprung, belly well drawn up. Back and loins strong, latter slightly arched.

Hindquarters

Extremely muscular, giving strength and galloping power. Second thigh long and well developed, good turn of stifle, hocks set low, turning neither in nor out.

Feet

Cat-like, turning neither in nor out. Toes well arched and close, nails strong and curved. Nails preferably dark in all coat colours, except harlequins, where light are permissible.

Tail

Thick at the root, tapering towards end, reaching to or just below hocks. Carried in straight line level with back, when dog is moving, slightly curved towards end, but never curling or carried over back.

Gait/Movement

Action lithe, springy and free, covering ground well. Hocks move freely with driving action, head carried high.

Coat

Short dense and sleek-looking, never inclined to roughness.

Colour

Brindles: must be striped, ground colour from lightest buff to deepest orange, stripes always black, eyes and nails preferably dark, dark shadings on head and ears acceptable. **Fawns**: colour varies from lightest buff to deepest orange, dark shadings on head and ears acceptable, eyes and nails preferably dark. **Blues**: colour varies from light grey to deep slate, the nose and eyes may be blue. **Blacks**: black is black. In all above colours white is only permissible on chest and feet, but it is not desirable even there. Nose always black, except in blues and harlequins. Eyes and nails preferably dark. **Harlequins**: pure white underground with preferably all black patches or all blue patches, having appearance of being torn. Light nails permissible. In harlequins, wall eyes, pink noses, or butterfly noses permissible but not desirable.

Weight and Size

Minimum height of an adult dog over eighteen months: 76cms (30in), bitches 71cm (28in). Weight, minimum weight over eighteen months: dogs 54kg (120lb), bitches 46kg (100lb).

Faults

Any departure from the foregoing points should be considered a fault and the seriousness with which the fault should be regarded should be in exact proportion to its degree.

Note   Male animals should have two apparently normal testicles fully descended into the scrotum.

Interpretation of the UK Breed Standard

To clarify it we will now go through each section step by step in an attempt to familiarize you with it and help you picture the Great Dane as he is described in the UK Standard.

General Appearance

This is fairly self-explanatory. A Great Dane is a dog of majestic beauty combined with enormous substance. He should be able to carry his head proudly with the desired long reach of neck that helps to enhance this point. His body should be solid, muscular, fit, and, combined with these three points, elegant. There should be no degree of coarseness throughout. The dog's tail should, when on the move, preferably be in line with the back; if it is slightly raised from this position it is just about acceptable, but at no time should it be at such a point where it is over the back and hindquarters.

*International Champion Eick
Imperial.*

Characteristics

The Great Dane should have an alert expression, and encompassed in the physical being of the dog should be an impression of strength and power. As well as these attributes there should also be a degree of dignity. As you know, the Dane is renowned for his height and substance, and together with this you should also be able to discern the regal character that has been handed down over the centuries from his ancestors. One of the fondest terms a Dane is known by is the Apollo of the dog world, and this title seems to sum the dog up as he truly is.

Temperament

'Kindly without nervousness, friendly and outgoing' is what the Standard requires. In any breed there is nothing worse than a shrinking violet and in the Great Dane it seems even worse. On the other hand, you do not wish to have an over-exuberant aggressive dog either. Although it is generally believed to be true that a great show dog is born and cannot be made, with the correct handling, rearing and love there is no excuse for your Dane to be anything other than a friendly and easily manageable dog. Of course, there are always exceptions to any rule, but I maintain that with plenty of good rearing combined with a lot of attention during the first few months of his life, your dog should live up to the animal described within this section of the Standard.

Head and Skull

The head of a Great Dane should give the impression of containing within it a balance of even proportions. The muzzle needs to be broad while the upper part of the head should in fact be narrow in proportion. When you view the head of the Great Dane from directly in front,

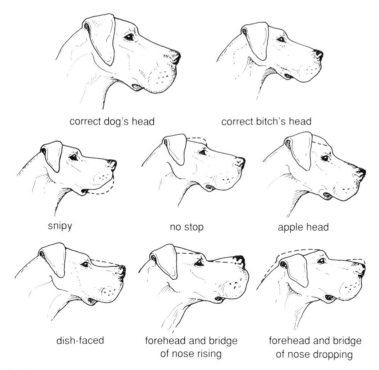

correct dog's head   correct bitch's head

snipy   no stop   apple head

dish-faced   forehead and bridge   forehead and bridge
of nose rising   of nose dropping

The head.

25

you should be able to see the head in equal proportions throughout the body. The Standard states: 'length of head in proportion to height of dog'. This is exactly as it sounds and is a visual thing – in its dimensions it should look exactly right!

Let us now assume you are looking at the head once more, this time from the side. You should see that the dog's head is in equal proportions of length. That is, from the tip of his nose to the slight rise in the outline, or bridge, should be the same distance as it is from there to the back of the dog's head or the 'occiput'. Now look at the area from the 'bridge' or 'rise' back towards the neck. This should be flat but when you look at it from either the front of the dog or above you should be able to see the desired indentation running up the centre of the skull. As called for, the point at the back of the dog's head, the occiputal peak, should not be too pronounced.

Let us return to viewing the dog from the side. You should be able to see near the area of the eyes a slight but definite rise in the outline. As you will see if you refer to pages 20–1, this is all that is called for; there is no definite stop as with some other breeds. This rise is the point where the cartilage is joined to the bone and gives this 'finish'.

'Face well chiselled': this is quite straightforward and really means as it sounds. The outline and area of the head should be clear and defined. There should be no evidence of unevenness or excess of fat or skin. The area under the eyes should be well filled so that you get neither the impression of 'puffiness' nor a snipey, mean or sharp expression. Looking at the outline of the head once more, but this time concentrating more on the line running underneath the skull and foreface, this should appear, as near as possible, straight. You should be able to see a line from the corner of the lip extending to the corner of the jawbone. However, the Standard does allow for a fold of the lip but also demands that there should be no excess of loose skin hanging down.

The nostrils of the dog should be 'large, wide and open' and this should also help to give the impression of the desired 'blunt look' to the nose.

Looking at the dog's head from the front, you should see that the lips hang down squarely, giving an impression of being at a right angle to the upper line of the foreface.

Eyes

They should preferably be dark and should be set in to the skull fairly deeply and be evenly placed. They should not give the impression of

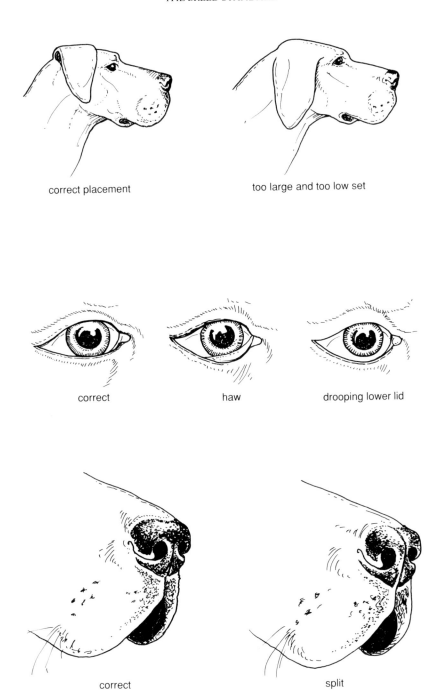

correct placement

too large and too low set

correct

haw

drooping lower lid

correct

split

The ears, eyes and nose.

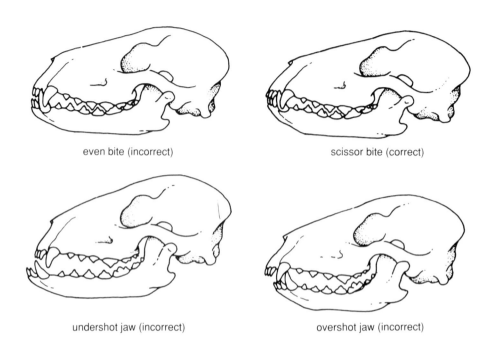

even bite (incorrect)　　　　　　　　scissor bite (correct)

undershot jaw (incorrect)　　　　　　overshot jaw (incorrect)

The jaw.

being round. The eyelids, in fact, should almost be almond shaped. In harlequins, dark eyes are also desirable but in this colour the Standard does allow 'wall eyes' or 'odd eyes' also.

Ears

The ears of the Great Dane should be triangular and should be set on to the skull at the correct angle, that is high rather than low, and should preferably fall slightly forward. The ear of the Dane should be neat; I do not mean small when I say this, but, on the other hand, they should not appear to be long and pendulous giving an appearance of a blood-hound.

Mouth

The Standard calls for the scissor bite. Translated, this means that the upper set of teeth should close slightly over the front of the bottom teeth. The teeth also need to be level and the jaws strong. Teeth are an important feature of this breed, especially on the Continent. Now we all know that a dog does not walk on his teeth, and to damn a dog for perhaps one fault is in my opinion fault-judging, but good dentition is sought after, and it could be that an otherwise lovely dog could have his chances blighted on some occasions by the lack of this. So you should take notice of your dog's teeth and care for them.

Neck

The neck should be long and clean cut with a good reach. It should also be well arched, enhancing that nobility so apparent in the Dane. The arch should rise up in a slight curve towards the back of the head where it meets the neck and should be well defined. At the base of the neck it should meld beautifully into the rest of the body while giving an appearance of strength and fitness. The neck should carry the head proudly and should have clean lines, free of flabby skin.

Forequarters

The shoulders of the Dane should be set well into the body, sloping slightly backwards; the elbows should be set well under the body and should not on any account extend outwards. The shoulders should also be well covered and muscular. The actual shoulder blade should not be set too steeply into the body, nor should it appear to be over-angulated.

Below the shoulder setting, the dog's forelegs should give the desired appearance of being straight with long flat bones when viewed from the front. You should not be able to see any evidence of bowing or any weakness at all. One must remember that the Great Dane needs to be constructed especially well here (as should any dog, of course), but particularly so with a Dane. He needs four good strong legs to be able to carry his large frame with ease and soundness.

Body

The body needs to be deep, very deep in fact, with plenty of room

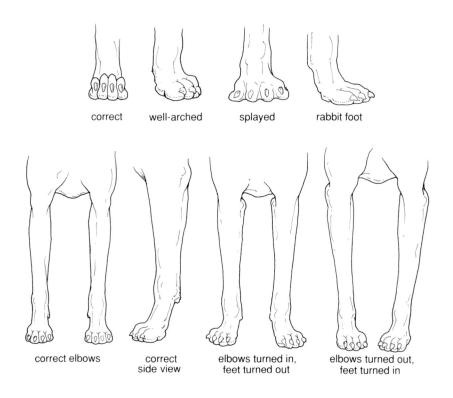

correct   well-arched   splayed   rabbit foot

correct elbows   correct
side view   elbows turned in,
feet turned out   elbows turned out,
feet turned in

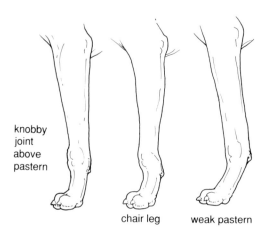

knobby
joint
above
pastern

chair leg   weak pastern

Forequarters and feet.

available for the lungs and heart so that they can work with ease. This is the reason that these ribs should be well sprung. The body shape should be constructed so that the dog can have all his important organs working in the way that enabled his forefathers to do a good day's work on the hunting field. Of course, there is no suggestion that you are about to go hunting wild boar in the local park, but there is no excuse for the Dane not to be bred in the same correct and proper manner. If you think about it logically, in a dog that is slab-sided (i.e. where the ribs appear to be practically straight and narrowing in under the dog's chest), where is the desired space for the all-important organs? Their working capacity will be restricted and in turn limit the working power of the dog. Another point regarding an incorrectly formed rib-cage is the fact that it can put out of line other skeletal features, which will take many years even to attempt to breed out.

For instance, the Standard states that the brisket should be deep enough to reach the elbows. If the body is incorrectly formed, for example say the dog in question is slab-sided, it would be difficult for this point required by the Standard to be attained. If it was, can you imagine how severely restricted the inner body region would be? Body formation and skeletal structure are extremely important and you owe it to your future dogs' good health to try to achieve this by breeding in the correct manner.

The underneath or belly of the Dane should be drawn well up when you are viewing it from the side, and it is decreed that the back and loins should be strong. You should not have a 'whippet' look, that is lighter behind than in front. If your dog has the correct body, it must be well balanced to enable the dog to move smoothly and easily. There is no point in having the required solidity of body on light-boned fore- and hindquarters. Finally, the back of the Dane should be slightly arched.

Hindquarters

As I have just mentioned with the forelegs in the preceding paragraph, the hindquarters should be strong; in fact, the Standard is quite explicit: 'extremely muscular, giving strength and galloping power'. The rest of the definition is quite clear: it asks for the 'second thigh long and well developed, good turn of stifle, hocks set low, turning neither in nor out'. When viewed from behind you should be able to see that the back legs are evenly placed and that they show no signs of weakness

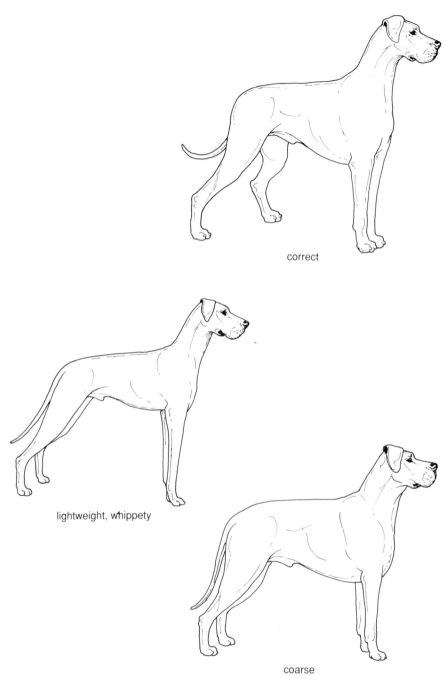

correct

lightweight, whippety

coarse

Body shape.

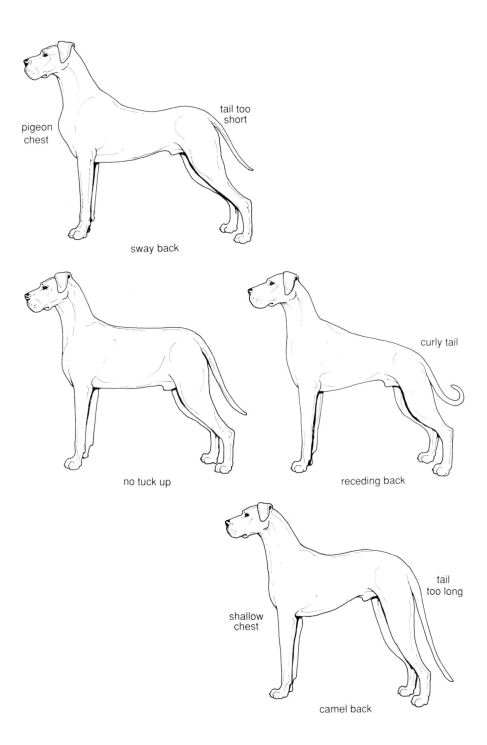

pigeon chest

tail too short

sway back

no tuck up

curly tail

receding back

shallow chest

tail too long

camel back

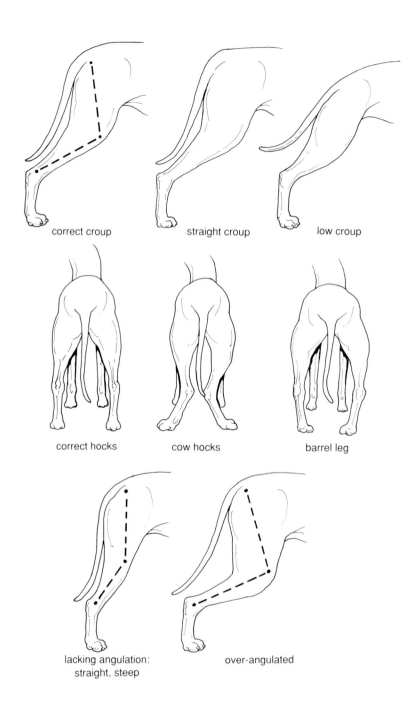

correct croup

straight croup

low croup

correct hocks

cow hocks

barrel leg

lacking angulation:
straight, steep

over-angulated

Hindquarters.

whatsoever. There should be no evidence either of 'cowhocks' (i.e. when the legs bend inwards), or of the legs bending outwards. Both are bad faults, for a dog of this size and build would be unable to move comfortably if he was expected to carry himself on limbs as weakly and badly constructed as this.

Feet

The feet of the Dane should be 'cat-like' and of course it goes without saying that these should turn neither inwards nor outwards. The toes should be well covered and the foot in no way should be 'splayed'. However, do not throw yourself into a fit of panic if a young puppy during its teething and early growth period shows these signs. At this stage of its development, the feet, amongst other things, can do strange things, but eventually you hope that they come up to the formation that the Standard asks for.

It is vital that from an early age your Dane puppy gets used to a regular manicure (this will be covered more fully in Chapter 4, *see* page 81). If the dog's nails are allowed to become too long this will throw the foot out of the desired shape, apart from the fact that it is uncomfortable for the dog and unsightly also. It is preferred that the nails should be dark; however, in harlequins lighter-coloured nails are permitted.

Gait/Movement

'Action, lithe springy and free.' The Dane should have a movement that gives an impression of ease. When coming towards, his action should be true. On no account should there by any sign of pacing which gives an ungainly and unbalanced action and is totally incorrect. The dog should be able to cover the ground freely, assisted by a strong driving movement from behind. While the dog is in motion the head should be carried high and proud, giving the desired impression of a majestic animal.

Tail

The tail of a Dane should be thicker at the root than at the tip and should taper neatly down to the end. It should reach to, or to just below, the hocks. A Dane's tail is easily damaged, very often by sheer over-exuberance. Your dog may be so pleased to see you that his tail gets carried away in a welcome and can easily hit a sharp or hard

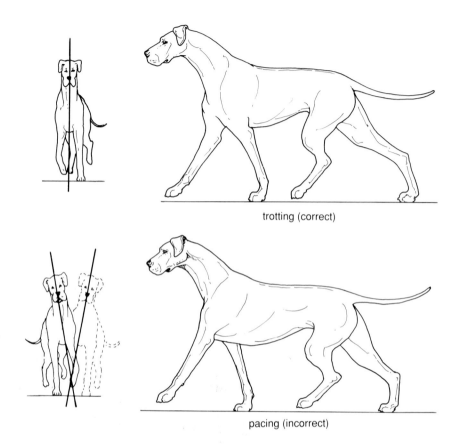

trotting (correct)

pacing (incorrect)

Gait.

object, damaging the tail in the process and possibly leaving an unsightly scar. While on the subject of tails, I would advise you to place any of your valuable ornaments high out of harm's way!

On the move, the tail should be seen to be carried in a line with the back. When you are viewing the dog from the side it should reach out and is allowed to curve slightly up at the end. On no account should it curve over the dog's back, nor should it have any curl in it.

Coat

The coat should be short and have a density to it; the appearance of it should be sleek and should never feel rough to the touch.

Colour

The various colours of the Great Dane are as stated: brindles, fawns, blues, blacks and harlequins. Once again the definitions for these colours are quite clear as set out within the Standard.

Weight

The Standard states a minimum weight and size from the age of eighteen months. The male is, as you would expect, larger than the female. The Standard requires the male to be no less than 76cm (30in) and the weight to be no lighter than 54kg (120lb), while for the female the lower height is 71cm (28in), with the minimum weight being set at 46kg (100lb).

As with all Breed Standards within the UK it also requires that the dogs should be fully entire and that the two testicles should be fully descended into the scrotum; in other words, that both testicles are in the sac. This does not allow for a 'floater' or one of the testicles alternating between being in and out of the sac.

Two further Breed Standards follow: one for the German Great Dane, submitted by the Deutsche Doggen Club, and the other for the American Great Dane, as submitted by the Kennel Club of America. So here we have the three Standards by which the Great Dane is assessed throughout the world. Regardless of where you show or breed Great Danes, it helps to study all three Standards and compare them, as this will enable you to develop a deeper understanding of the breed's characteristics.

How, you are probably asking yourself, do you come to own a dog that fits the Standard exactly? The answer is that you will probably never find a dog or bitch that fits the Standard absolutely word for word. The essence of breeding and responsible breeding is that you should aspire to produce as near a perfect specimen as possible.

Remember every dog has at least one fault and, providing that fault is not a horrendous one, keep it in mind but do not be blinded by it. Remember all your dog's good points as well. Try not to be negative when comparing your Dane with the Standard, for he will most likely possess good qualities that can make up for one minor fault. It is the seriousness of the fault that matters most, and the number of them!

The American Breed Standard

(Reproduced by kind permission of the American Kennel Club)

1   General Conformation

(a) General Appearance

The Great Dane combines in its distinguished appearance dignity, strength and elegance with great size and a powerful, well-formed, smoothly muscled body. He is one of the giant breeds, but is unique in that his general conformation must be so well balanced that he never appears clumsy and is always a unit – the Apollo of dogs. He must be spirited and courageous – never timid. He is friendly and dependable. This physical and mental combination is the characteristic which gives the Great Dane the majesty possessed by no other breed. It is particularly true of this breed and there is an impression of great masculinity in dogs as compared to an impression of femininity in bitches. The male should appear more massive throughout than the bitch, with larger frame and heavier bone. In the ratio between length and height, the Great Dane should appear as square as possible. In bitches, a somewhat longer body is permissible. *Faults* – Lack of unity; timidity; bitchy dogs; poor musculature; poor bone development; out of condition, rickets; doggy bitches.

(b) Color and Marking

(i) **Brindle Danes**. Base color ranging from light golden yellow to deep golden yellow always brindled with strong black cross stripes; deep-black mask preferred. Black may or may not appear on the eyes, ears and tail tip. The more intensive the base color and the more distinct the brindling, the more attractive will be the color. Small white marks at the chest and toes are not desirable. *Faults* – Brindle with too dark a base color; silver-blue and grayish-blue base color; dull (faded) brindlings; white tail tip. Black fronted, dirty colored brindles are not desirable.

(ii) **Fawn Danes**. Light golden yellow to deep golden yellow color with a deep black mask. Black may or may not appear on the eyes, ears, and tail tip. The deep golden yellow color must always be given the preference. Small white spots at the chest and toes are not desirable. *Faults* – Yellowish-gray, bluish-yellow, grayish-blue, dirty yellow color (drab color), lack of black mask. Black fronted, dirty colored fawns are not desirable.

(iii) **Blue Danes**. The color must be a pure steel blue, as far as possible without any tinge of yellow, black or mouse gray. Small white marks at the chest and toes are not desirable. *Faults* – Any deviation from a pure steel-blue coloration.

(iv) **Black Dane**. Glossy black. *Faults* – Yellow-black, brown-black or blue-black. White markings, such as stripes on the chest, speckled chest and markings on the paws are permitted but not desirable.

(v) **Harlequin Danes**. Base color: pure white with black torn patches irregularly and well distributed over the entire body; pure white neck preferred. The black patches should never be large enough to give the appearance of a blanket nor so small as to give a stippled or dappled effect. (Eligible, but less desirable, are a few small gray spots; also pointings where instead of a pure white base with black spots, there is a white base with single black hairs showing through which tend to give a salt and pepper or dirty effect.) *Faults* – White base color with a few large spots; bluish-gray pointed background.

(c) Size

The male should be less than 30 inches [76cm] at the shoulders, but it is preferable that he be 32 inches [81cm] or more, providing he is well proportioned to his height. The female should not be less than 28 inches [71cm] at the shoulders, but it is preferable that she be 30 inches or more, providing she is well proportioned to her height.

(d) Condition of Coat

The coat should be very short and thick, smooth, and glossy. *Faults* – Excessively long hair (stand-off coat); dull hair (indicating malnutrition, worms and negligent care).

(e) Substance

Substance is that sufficiency of bone and muscle which rounds out a balance with the frame. *Faults* – Lightweight whippety Danes; coarse, ungainly proportioned Danes – always there should be balance.

2 Movement

(a) Gait

Long, easy, springy stride with no tossing or rolling of body. The back line should move smoothly, parallel to the ground, with minimum rise and fall. The gait of the Great Dane should denote strength and power showing good driving action in the hindquarters and good reach in front. As speed increases, there is a natural tendency for the legs to converge toward the center line of balance beneath the body and there should be no twisting in or out at the joints. *Faults* – Interference or crossing; twisting joints; short steps; stilted steps; the rear quarters should not pitch; the forelegs should not have a hackney gait. When moving rapidly, the Great Dane should not pace for the reason that it causes excessive side-to-side rolling of the body and thus reduces endurance.

(b) Rear End (Croup, Legs, Paws)

The croup must be full, slightly drooping and must continue imperceptibly to the tail root. *Faults* – A croup which is too straight; a croup which slopes downward too steeply; and too narrow a croup. Hind legs, the first thighs (from hip joint to knee) are broad and muscular. The second thighs (from knee to hock joint) are strong and long. Seen from the side, the angulation of the first thigh with the body, of the second thigh with the first thigh, and the pastern root with the second thigh should be very moderate, neither too straight nor too exaggerated. Seen from the rear, the hock joints appear to be perfectly straight, turned neither towards the inside nor towards the outside. *Faults* – Hind legs: Soft flabby, poorly muscled thighs; cowhocks which are the result of the hock joint turning inward and the hock and rear paws turning outward; barrel legs, the result of the hock joints being too far apart; steep rear. As seen from the side, a steep rear is the result of the angles of the rear legs forming almost a straight line; overangulation is the result of exaggerated angles between the first and second thighs and the hocks and is very conducive to weakness. The rear legs should never be too long in proportion to the front legs.

Paws – Round and turned neither toward the inside nor toward the outside. Toes short, highly arched and well closed. Nails short, strong and as dark as possible. *Faults* – Spreading toes (splay foot); bent, long toes (rabbit paws); toes turned toward the outside or toward the inside. Furthermore, the fifth toe on the hind legs appearing at a higher position and with wolf's claw or spur; excessively long nails; light-colored nails.

(c) Front End (Shoulders, Legs, Paws)

Shoulders – The shoulder blades must be strong and sloping and seen from the side must form as nearly as possible a right angle in its articulation with the humerus (upper arm) to give a long stride. A line from the upper tip of the shoulder to the back of the elbow joint should be as

40

nearly perpendicular as possible. Since all dogs lack a clavicle (collar bone) the ligaments and muscles holding the shoulder blade to the rib cage must be well developed, firm and secure to prevent loose shoulders. *Faults* – Steep shoulders, which occur if the shoulder blade does not slope sufficiently; overangulation; loose shoulders which occur if the Dane is flabby muscled, or if the elbow is turned toward the outside; loaded shoulders.

Forelegs – The upper arm should be strong and muscular. Seen from the side or front, the strong lower arms run absolutely straight to the pastern joints. Seen from the front, the forelegs and the pastern roots should form perpendicular lines to the ground. Seen from the side, the pastern root should slope only very slightly forward. *Faults* – Elbows turned toward the inside or toward the outside, the former position caused mostly by too narrow or too shallow a chest, bringing the front legs too closely together and at the same time turning the entire lower part of the leg outward; the latter position causes the front legs to spread too far apart, with the pastern roots and paws usually turned inwards. Seen from the side, a considerable bend in the pastern toward the front indicates weakness and is in most cases connected with stretched and spread toes (splay foot); seen from the side, a forward bow in the forearm (chair leg); an excessively knotty bulge in the front of the pastern joint.

Paws – Round and turned neither toward the inside nor toward the outside. Toes short, highly arched and well closed. Nails short, strong and as dark as possible. *Faults* – Spreading toes (splay foot), bent, long toes (rabbit paws); toes turned toward the outside or toward the inside; light-colored nails.

3   Head

(a) Head Conformation

Long, narrow, distinguished, expressive, finely chiseled, especially the part below the eyes (which means that the skull plane under and to the inner point of the eye must slope without any bony protuberance in a pleasing line to the full square jaw), with strongly pronounced stop. The masculinity of the male is very pronounced in the expression and structure of head (this subtle difference should be evident in the dog's head through massive skull and depth of muzzle); the bitch's head may be more delicately formed. Seen from the side, the forehead must be sharply set off from the bridge of the nose. The forehead and the bridge of the nose must be straight and parallel to one another. Seen from the front, the head should appear narrow, the bridge of the nose should be as broad as possible. The cheek muscles must show slightly, but under no circumstances should they be too pronounced (cheeky). The muzzle part must have full flews and must be as blunt vertically as possible in front; the angles of the lips must be quite pronounced. The front part of the head, from the tip of the nose up to the center of the stop should be as long as the rear part of the head from the center of the stop to the only slightly developed occiput. The head should be angular from all sides and should have definite flat planes and its dimensions should be absolutely in proportion to the general appearance of the Dane. *Faults* – Any deviation from the parallel planes of skull and foreface; too small a stop; a poorly defined stop or none at all; too narrow a nose bridge; the rear of the head spreading laterally in a wedgelike manner (wedge head); an excessively round upper head (apple head); excessively pronounced cheek musculature; pointed muzzle; loose lips hanging over the lower jaw (fluttering lips) which create an illusion of a full deep muzzle. The head should be rather shorter and distinguished than long and expressionless.

(b) Teeth
Strong, well developed and clean. The incisors of the lower jaw must touch very lightly the bottoms of the inner surface of the upper incisors (scissors bite). If the front teeth of both jaws bite on top of each other, they wear down too rapidly. *Faults* – Even bite; undershot and overshot; incisors out of line; black or brown teeth; missing teeth.

(c) Eyes
Medium size, as dark as possible, with lively intelligent expression; almond-shaped eyelids, well-developed eyebrows. *Faults* – Light-colored, piercing, amber-colored, light blue to a watery blue, red or bleary eyes; eyes of different colors; eyes too far apart; Mongolian eyes; eyes with pronounced haws; eyes with excessively drooping lower eyelids. In blue and black Danes, lighter eyes are permitted but are not desirable. In harlequins, the eyes should be dark. Light-colored eyes, two eyes of different color and wall eyes are permitted but not desirable.

(d) Nose
The nose must be large and in the case of brindled and 'single-colored' Danes, it must always be black. In harlequins, the nose should be

black; a black spotted nose is permitted; a pink-colored nose is not desirable.

(e) Ears
Ears should be high, set not too far apart, medium in size, of moderate thickness, drooping forward close to the cheek. Top line of folded ear should be about level with the skull. *Faults* – Hanging on the side, as on a Foxhound. **Cropped ears:** high set, not set too far apart, well pointed but always in proportion to the shape of the head and carried uniformly erect.

4 Torso

(a) Neck
The neck should be firm and clean, high-set, well arched, long, muscular and sinewy. From the chest to the head, it should be slightly tapering, beautifully formed, with well-developed nape. *Faults* – Short, heavy neck, pendulous throat folds (dewlaps).

(b) Loin and Back
The withers form the highest part of the back which slopes downward slightly toward the loins which are imperceptibly arched and strong. The back should be short and tensely set. The belly should be well shaped and tightly muscled, and, with the rear part of the thorax, should swing in a pleasing curve (tuck-up). *Faults* – Receding back; sway back; camel or roach back; a back line which is too high at the rear; an excessively long back; poor tuck-up.

(c) Chest
Chest deals with that part of the thorax (rib cage) in front of the shoulders and front legs. The chest should be quite broad, deep and well muscled. *Faults* – A narrow and poorly muscled chest; strong protruding sternum (pigeon breast).

(d) Ribs and Brisket
Deals with that part of the thorax back of the shoulders and front legs. Should be broad, with the ribs sprung well from the spine and flattened at the side to allow proper movement of the shoulders extending down to the elbow joint. *Faults* – Narrow (slab-sided) rib cage; round (barrel) rib cage; shallow rib cage not reaching the elbow joint.

5 Tail

Should start high and fairly broad, terminating slender and thin at the hock joint. At rest, the tail should fall straight. When excited or running, slightly curved (saberlike). *Faults* – A too high, or too low set tail (the tail set is governed by the slope of the croup); too long or too short a tail; tail bent too far over the back (ring tail); a tail which is curled; a twisted tail (sideways); a tail carried too high over the back (gay tail); a brush tail (hair too long on lower side). Cropping tails to desired length is forbidden.

Disqualifications

Danes under minimum height.
White Danes without any black marks (albinos).
Merles, a solid mouse-gray color or a mouse-gray base with black or white or both color spots or white base with mouse-gray spots.
Harlequins and solid-colored Danes in which a large spot extends coatlike over the entire body so that only the legs, neck and the point of the tail are white.
Brindle, fawn, blue and black Danes with white forehead line, white collars, high white stockings and white bellies.
Danes with predominantly blue, gray, yellow or also brindled spots.
Any color other than those described under 'Color and Markings.'
Docked tails.
Split noses.

Approved 10 August 1976

The German Great Dane Standard

(Reproduced by kind permission of the Deutsche Doggen Club)

General Appearance and Character

The Great Dane combines pride, strength and elegance in its noble appearance and big, strong, well-coupled body. It is the Apollo of all the breeds of dog. The Dane strikes one by its very expressive head; it does not show any nervousness even in the greatest excitement, and has the appearance of a noble statue. In temperament it is friendly, loving and affectionate with its masters, especially with children, but retiring and mistrustful with strangers. In time of danger the dog is courageous and not afraid of attacks, caring only for the defense of its master and the latter's property.

Head

Elongated, narrow, striking, full of expression, finely chiselled (especially the part under the eyes), with strongly accentuated stop. Seen from the side, the brow should be sharply broken off from the bridge of the nose. The forehead and bridge of the nose must run into each other in a straight and parallel line. Seen from the front, the head must appear narrow, the bridge of the nose must be as broad as possible; the cheek muscles should be only slightly accentuated, but in no case must they be prominent. The muzzle must be full of lip, as much as possible vertically blunted in front, and show well-accentuated lip-angle. The underjaw should be neither protruding nor retrograding.

The forehead, from the tip of the nose to the stop, must as far as possible be of the same length as the back of the head, from the stop to the slightly accentuated occiput. Seen from all sides, the head should appear angular and settled in its outer lines, but at the same time it should harmonize entirely with the general appearance of the Great Dane in every way. *Faults* – Falling-off line of brow, an elevated, falling-off or compressed bridge of nose; too little or no stop; too narrow a bridge of nose; the back of the head wedge-shaped; too round a skull (apple head); cheeks too pronounced; snipy muzzle. Also loose lips hanging over the underjaw, which can be deceptive as to a full, deep muzzle. It is preferable for the head to be short and striking, rather than long, shallow and expressionless.

Eyes

Of medium size, round, as dark as possible, with gay, hearty expression, the eyebrows well developed. *Faults* – Eyes light, cutting, amber-yellow, light blue or water blue, or of two different colours; too low-hanging eyelids with prominent tear glands or very red conjunctiva tunica.

Ears

Set on high, not too far apart, of good length, cropped to a point. *Faults* – Ears set on too low, laterally; cropped too short or not uniformly;

standing too much over or even lying on the head; not carried erect or semi-drooping ears. (Uncropped Danes should not win.) (*Translator's note*: Of course the above refers to cropped ears; in the UK, the ears should be small.)

Nose

Large, black, running in a straight line with the bridge. *Faults* – Nose light coloured, with spots, or cleft.

Teeth

Large and strong, white, fitting into each other, which is correct when the lower incisors fit tightly into the upper ones just as two scissor blades. *Faults* – The incisors of the lower jaw are protruding (undershot) or those of the upper jaw protrude (overshot). Also, when the incisors of both jaws stand one upon another ('crackers'), for in this case the teeth wear out prematurely. Imperceptible deviations are allowed. Distemper teeth should be objected to as they hide caries; likewise when the teeth look broken or are brown. Tartar is also undesirable.

Neck

Long, dry, muscular and sinewy, without strongly developed skin or dewlap; it should taper slightly from the chest to the head, be nicely ascending, and set on high with a well-formed nape. *Faults* – Neck short, thick with loose skin or dewlap.

Shoulders

The shoulder-blade should be long and slanting; it should join the bone of the upper arm in the same position in the shoulder joint, as far as possible forming a right angle, in order to allow roomy movement. The withers should be well accentuated. *Faults* – Straight or loose shoulders; the former occur when the shoulder-blade is not sufficiently slanting, the latter when the elbows turn outwards.

Chest

As large as possible, the ribs well rounded, deep in front, reaching up to the elbow joints. *Faults* – Chest narrow, shallow with flat ribs; chest bone protruding too much.

Body

The back straight, short and tight, the body should be as far as possible square in relation to the height; a somewhat longer back is allowed in bitches. The loins should be lightly arched and strong, the croup running fully imperceptibly into the root of the tail. The belly should be well tucked up backwards, and forming a nicely arched line with the inside of the chest. *Faults* – Saddle-back, roach-back, or when the height of the hindquarters exceeds that of the forequarters (overbuilt); too long a back, since the gait then suffers (rolling gait); the croup falling off at a slant; belly hanging down and badly showing teats in bitches.

Tail

Of medium length, only reaching to the hocks, set on high and broad, but tapering to a point; hanging down straight at rest, slightly curved (sword-like) in excitement or in running, not carried over the back. *Faults* – Tail too long, too low set on, carried too high over the back, or curled over the back; turned sideways; broken off or docked (it is forbidden to shorten the tail to obtain the prescribed length); brush tail (when the hair on the inside is too long) is undesirable. It is forbidden to shave the tail.

Front legs

The continuation of the elbows of the forearm must not reach the round of the chest, but must be well let down, must not appear either inwards or outwards, but should lie in equal flatness with the shoulder joint. The upper arms should be strong, broad and muscular, the legs strong and – seen from the front or the side – absolutely straight down to the pasterns. *Faults* – Elbows turning in or out; if turning in, their position impedes movement by rubbing against the ribs, and at the same time turns the whole lower part of the legs and causes the feet to turn outwards; if turning out, the reverse happens and the toes are forced inwards. Both these positions are at fault, but the latter does not hinder movement since it does not cause any rubbing of the elbows against the chest wall. If the forelegs stand too wide apart the feet are forced to turn inwards, while in the case of the 'narrow' stand brought about by the narrow chest, the front legs incline towards each other and the toes again turn outwards. The curving of the joint of the root of the front foot is equally faulty; it points to weakness in the pasterns (soft pasterns) or in foot-roots (tarsus), and often causes flat feet and splayed toes. Swelling over the joint of the tarsus points mainly to diseases of the bone (rickets).

Hind Legs

The buttocks of the hind legs should be broad and muscular. The under-thighs long, strong, and forming a not too obtuse angle with the short tarsus. Seen from behind, the hocks should appear absolutely straight, sloping neither outwards nor inwards. *Faults* – If the knee-joint is turned too far outwards, the under-thigh forces the hock inwards and the dog is then 'cowhocked,' not a nice position at all. Too broad a stand in the hocks is just as ugly, as it impedes the light move-ment. In profile, the well-developed hind thigh shows good angula-tion. A straight hind thigh is faulty, for there the under-thigh is too short and the dog is forced to keep it vertically to the straight tarsus. If the bone of the hind thighs is too long (in relation to the forelimbs) then the hind thighs are diagonally bent together, and this is not at all good.

Feet

Roundish, turned neither inwards nor outwards. The toes should be short, highly arched and well closed, the nails short, strong and black. *Faults* – Splayed toes, hare-feet, toes turned inwards or outwards; fur-ther, the fifth toes on the hind legs placed higher (dew claw); also if the nails are too long, or light in colour.

Movement

Fleeting, stepping out. *Faults* – Short strides which are not free; narrow or rolling gait; ambling gait.

Coat

Very short and thick, lying close and shiny. *Faults* – Hair too long; lopped hair (due to bad feeding, worms and faulty care).

Colour

(a) Brindle Danes

Ground colour from light golden fawn to dark golden fawn, always with well-defined black stripes. The more intense the ground colour and the stronger the stripes, the more striking is the effect. Small white patches on the chest and toes, or light eyes and nails, are not desirable. *Faults* – Silver-blue or biscuit-coloured ground colour, washed-out stripes, white streak between the eyes up to the nose, white ring on the neck, white 'socks' and white tip of tail. Danes with such white markings should be excluded from winning prizes.

(b) Fawn Danes

Colour, fawn-golden and fawn to dark golden fawn; black mask as well as black nails are desired. The golden-fawn colour should always be preferred. *Faults* – Silver-grey, blue-grey, biscuit-fawn and dirty-fawn colour should be placed lower in the award list. For white markings, *see* (a) above. (*Translator's note*: It will be seen that whereas a black mask in fawn Great Danes was formerly not desired, as reminding one of Mastiffs, it is now desired.)

(c) Blue Danes

The colour should be as far as possible steel blue, without any tinge of fawn or black. Lighter eyes are allowed in blue Danes. *Faults* – Fawn-blue or black-blue colour, too light or wall eyes. Regarding white markings, *see* (a) above.

(d) Black Danes

Should be wallflower black, shiny, with dark eyes and black nails. *Faults* – Yellow-brown or blue-black colour; light or amber-coloured eyes; lightly coloured nails. Danes with too many white markings should be lower in the list of awards. Under white markings it should be noted that a white streak on the throat, spots on the chest, on toes (only up the pasterns) are allowed, but Danes with a white blaze, white ring on the neck, white 'socks' or white belly, should be debarred from winning.

(e) Harlequins

The ground colour should always be white, without any spots, with patches running all over the body, well-torn, irregular, wallflower black (a few small grey or brownish patches are admitted but not desired). Nose and nails should be black, but a nose with black spots or a fleshy nose are allowed. Eyes should be dark; light or two-coloured eyes are permitted but not desired. *Faults* – White ground colour with several large, black patches; bluish-grey ground colour; water-light, red or bleary eyes.

The following Danes should be excluded from winning:

1. White Danes without any black markings; albinos, as well as deaf Danes.
2. 'Mantle' harlequins, i.e. Danes having a large patch – like a mantle – running all over the body, and only the legs, neck and tip of the tail are white.
3. So-called 'porcelain' harlequins, i.e. Danes with mostly blue-grey, fawn or even brindle patches.

Size

The height at the shoulder should not be under 76cm (30in) but preferably should measure about 80cm ($31\frac{1}{2}$ in); in bitches, not under 70cm ($27\frac{1}{2}$ in) but preferably 75cm ($29\frac{1}{2}$ in) and over.

3

Buying Your Puppy

I would imagine that at this stage you have already decided that you wish to have a Great Dane. What is very important and should be given due consideration is, are you prepared to take on the responsibility involved in keeping a Dane and basically devote your life to its needs? Before answering 'yes' straightaway you must first weigh up all the pros and cons. You must remember that there is much more involved than just going to see a breeder and choosing an adorable and appealing puppy. You must bear in mind that this delightful bundle of joy is soon going to grow up into a 'large bundle of joy' that will give you headaches and cause problems if you are not fully prepared.

The Canine Defence League's slogan 'A Dog Is For Life, Not Just For Christmas' sums up dog ownership. When you buy a puppy, you must be prepared to accept that he will become a part of your life and your home. If you feel that you cannot make that commitment, you are best advised not to have a dog at all.

When I have an interested puppy buyer I advise them, when coming to see a litter, to look at my adults first; and also I personally like them to bring along their immediate family. There are two reasons for this. The first is so that I can meet them and talk about the dogs to see if they would be able to manage to care for and cope with rearing a Great Dane. Maybe not everyone in the family can even visualize the enormousness of a Great Dane, and it would be unfair of me to let them have a puppy that might eventually prove to be a problem for them.

The second reason is that I like to meet the children of the family, if there are any, to see how kind and gentle they are and how they respond to the dogs. If they are unruly, and their parents cannot control them, then they have no hope of learning to train and control a Great Dane, and I decline the sale on these grounds. How fair would it be to let a young puppy go to a home such as this and eventually, through mismanagement, end up as a poor unwanted creature in a rescue home? Not for them one of mine!

Showing

Another question is, are you buying this young puppy purely as a companion and pet? Or do you wish to have a Dane in order to become involved in the world of showing? It has not been unknown for someone to buy a Dane solely as a pet and then, perhaps while walking the dog or attending a training class , be talked into showing him.

Before you suddenly think that maybe you have a future champion on your hands, stop and think seriously for a while. It is hoped that you have bought your puppy from a caring and responsible breeder, who has sold you specifically what you asked for – a companion and pet. In a case such as this, your dog would have something in his make-up that precludes him from being successful in the ring. However, that does not detract from his faithfulness, his loving ways and the hours of wonderful enjoyment he will give you.

However, it has been known that a dog has been sold as a pet but as the months have passed any fault he possessed has diminished, or perhaps become less apparent due to his excelling in other regions. What I would suggest you do is to take your puppy, if at all possible, back to his breeder and ask their advice.

Two harlequin puppies.

A puppy must never be bought with the sole intention of making him a Champion. However, if you wish to buy a puppy for the show ring and know that, win or lose, you will be getting enormous enjoyment and pleasure out of being associated with this breed, then dog showing can provide endless fascination, at times despair and sometimes heartache together with a lot of fun. But, above all, it can immerse you into a lifetime of involvement with a very special dog.

Price

The amount you are likely to have to pay for a Great Dane depends very much on whether it is a prospective show puppy or not. Note that I always say 'prospective', for when you buy a puppy of this age you are taking a certain chance. Most breeders who have bred for many years know their lines, and they will know to the best of their ability how a puppy should turn out, but sometimes a fault may manifest itself at a later stage.

Two future Champions: Ch. Simba of Helmlake and Ch. Malindi of Helmlake taken at nine months.

A well-marked harlequin will always be more expensive than, say, a fawn, primarily because they are more difficult to breed. Prices can vary between breeders, and it sometimes depends in which part of the country the kennel is located. By and large, though, there is very little difference in this scale, and the money is far better paid to a reputable breeder for a well-reared and well-cared-for puppy, than spent on a cheaper one from somebody unaware how to breed and care for these lovely animals.

What many people are inclined to forget, or maybe perhaps do not realize, is the initial outlay that the owners of the dam have to contend with. There is the cost of travelling to a stud-dog plus the stud fee, when the dam's owner does not have a dog standing at stud or, for one reason or another, has used someone else's dog. As with anything, stud fees vary, dependent usually on the success of the dog, and especially of his progeny. In the UK, travelling to the stud-dog of your choice does not present too much of a problem. In the United States, distances are obviously far greater, and arrangements are indeed more complex than in Britain. The bitch needs to be transported, very often, to a dog many hundreds of miles away which in many cases necessitates the use of air travel. On top of this comes several weeks of constant care and attention, perhaps some veterinary fees, whelping and extra good food for the litter.

Finding a Reputable Breeder

There are two alternatives. The first choice you have is to ring the Kennel Club of your particular country, who will supply you with the name of a person in your area, in many cases it is the secretary of a Breed Club. This person will be able to put you in touch with somebody who may possibly have a litter of puppies at that particular time.

The other path you can follow is that of going to a show and seeing some of the dogs and breeders for yourself. In the UK, the two major dog journals are *Our Dogs* and *Dog World*, both easily obtainable from newsagents, who can easily order one or other for you. Both can be received outside the UK upon subscription. Each week both papers advertise forthcoming shows, from Championship Show level right down through the Open, Limited and finally Exemption Shows (I will explain the differences between each of these in Chapter 5, *see* pages 88–92). There are also Breed Club Shows which can fall into three categories; Championship, Limited and Open. This is where Great Danes

Danelaghs Eurus of Walkmyll.

will be the sole breed on show. There are also general All Breed Shows. Underneath the advertisement a name will be given, either that of the secretary or maybe the show manager. Contact this person and ask for a schedule and enquire as to the time of judging. Going to one of these shows is the best way of being introduced to the breed.

If you wish to buy a puppy that might develop into a show dog, I would suggest that you first look for an advertisement for an All Breed Championship Show or a Breed Club Show, if possible one within your area. At either of these shows you will see a fair representation of the different kennels throughout the country.

When you arrive at the show you will able to purchase a catalogue. At the All Breed Shows, look in the catalogue for directions to the Great Dane ring and also for the tent they are 'benched' in. This is where each dog is allotted a space on rows of partitioned, low-slung trestle tables. When you have reached the ring, watch the dogs being put through their paces, and see which ones appeal to you. Look specifically at the adults and you will start to see, the more you watch, that although they are all the same breed, many of them are different in outward appearances. Some are taller and more elegant than others,

Sarzec Blue Saxon taken at fourteen months.

while others are stockier with larger bone. Some may seem more exuberant in temperament with others appearing a little more withdrawn, a few may even seem to be nervous and perhaps fearful.

Watch the judge come to a decision and note which ones seem to be consistently up amongst the leaders. Watch as much of the judging as possible, try to attend at least another two shows before you make your decision. Judging can alter slightly from show to show and from judge to judge. However, a good dog or good breeding strain on most occasions will always come through and be among the leaders.

Take full advantage of your outings to the shows, and do not be afraid to approach any of the breeders whose dogs you admire (providing they are not about to step into the ring at the time). They will welcome your appreciation and in the vast majority of cases will be only too pleased to offer advice.

I would also advise you to go to as many kennels and breeders as you possibly can; there is no need to be in any hurry to buy the first puppy you see. Try to bear in mind that this new puppy is going to be a new member of your family, and, it is hoped, will be with you for a long time. Look first at the breeder's adults when you go: do you like

*Margaret Everton with Ch. Airways Wrangler, Int. and Nord. Ch.
Impton Duralex Berando and Ch. Impton Apache. (Photo. Pearce.)*

the type and look and, most important, do you also like their temperament? Also look at their condition: do they look well fed, cared for and
clean?

I personally think that this is a very important aspect of buying a
puppy. However, I hear cases of people trying to buy a puppy from
breeders who have never offered to show them anything other than
the puppy that is for sale. Instead, they were subjected to a hard-
pitched sales talk, encouraging them to buy this one puppy. All puppies of all breeds, whether they be pedigree or cross-bred, are
extremely adorable at this stage and I feel that the prospective
purchaser should be given a chance to see as much as possible, i.e. the
parents and, ideally, other adults and other puppies from the litter so
that they can compare. When offered just one puppy at this cuddly

Noah Le Mare with harlequin puppies.

and adorable age, few people are able to come away without this youngster, even when this may not be exactly what they wanted. I feel that for a prospective buyer to assess what a puppy is going to turn into, it is necessary for that person at least to be able to see some of his relations, a practice favoured by caring and responsible breeders. That is why I must stress, do not rush into this blindly, but look around, talk to breeders and learn and you will gradually come to know what you want.

When a puppy leaves my kennels, whether it be for the show ring or to a pet home, I always ask the new owners if they would bring the puppy back for me to see every four weeks. Just because the puppy has left my care does not mean that I am no longer interested in him. Being a breed that grows very quickly and needs to be on a careful and well-balanced diet, I think it is important to advise the new owner on the upbringing of the new puppy. Sometimes I may have to suggest that one meal is stepped up, or perhaps one other may be cut down. Each dog is different and that is why it is important, I feel, that someone who is experienced in this field should always be there to help. My door is never closed for advice, and if the puppy and owner do not live near then I try to ensure that a caring breeder who lives more locally will be there to help whenever necessary, or equally in case of an emergency.

Dog or Bitch?

I would advise that, in the vast majority of cases, a bitch puppy would be the best choice. In my experience there is nothing as sweet and gentle as a Great Dane bitch, especially when she reaches maturity. This does not mean that the males are any less delightful to own; the reason I suggest a bitch to many people if they are unsure is that the male is considerably larger than the female. The one disadvantage of a bitch is that she will come into season twice a year. If you do not intend to breed from her, you will be able to spay her when she is mature, thus preventing the problem, but until then you will have to ensure that she does not come into contact with males during the three weeks that she is in season. I usually find that someone coming to buy a male puppy from me has already set their heart on having a dog as opposed to a bitch. This is usually because they want their Dane to be large and masculine. Regarding the price of a puppy, unlike some breeds, there is no difference in the cost of buying a dog puppy as opposed to a bitch.

Choosing a Puppy

Let us assume that you have made all the relevant advances to a reputable breeder who has a litter of puppies and would be prepared to part with one of them. In many cases, depending on how many puppies the breeder has at that time, you may not always be able

NZ Ch. Helmlake Kaught in the Act (UK import), by Ch. Helmlake Implicable, ex Helmlake Jersey Fashion. Owned by Mr and Mrs J. Barkas, New Zealand..

to buy the pick of the litter, for the breeder, in order to keep and promote a good line, may well want to keep the pick of the puppies. That does not mean that you will not be able to obtain a really nice puppy, for in a well-bred litter all the puppies should be of a very high quality.

Registration

When a puppy is registered, the breeder will add his prefix to the dog's name. This prefix denotes the name of the kennel and breeder or strain. For instance, all puppies registered by me would carry the kennel name of Helmlake. Any puppy bred by me (that is out of a bitch registered and owned by me) will carry this name together with his registered Kennel Club name.

When a litter is registered with the Kennel Club the relevant paper work is sent off by the breeder to the Kennel Club with each puppy recorded, together with details of the sire and dam. The Kennel Club eventually approve or disallow these names. A second choice is always advisable for unless you make provision by doing this, or stating that you do not want the Kennel Club to choose a name for you, you may very well end up with a name that you cannot bear.

Therefore, when you buy your puppy the breeder will let you have a pedigree at the time together with the relevant recorded papers (if they have been received back from the Kennel Club). To transfer your Great Dane to your name, this form needs to be endorsed by both the breeder and you, and returned to the Kennel Club with the relevant fee.

4

Puppy and Adult Management

Compared with the normal life expectancy of a human, the span of years enjoyed by a dog is minimal, and therefore it is up to you to try to ensure that these years are stable and happy times for him.

Collecting the Puppy

On the day that you collect your puppy, I strongly recommend that someone comes with you, preferably someone who will drive while you hold and tend to your puppy who will be totally disorientated. The ride in the car will be a new experience for him and he will need you to give him some confidence and reassurance. Another tip is to make quite sure that you have some large towels to place on the seat or on your lap, in case the motion of the car causes the puppy to be sick.

The Puppy at Home

When you get your puppy home, allow him to become used to his new and strange surroundings gradually, letting him settle in to your way of life in his own way and his own time. The rearing of a puppy differs little from his human counterpart's. For when he has had an ample feed and has amused himself with a period of play, eventually tiredness will overcome him and he will want to lie down to sleep, probably on his own, in a quiet place. When a Dane puppy needs a sleep he must be allowed to do so away from the hustle and bustle of the household. He must never be annoyed or disturbed from his slumber by your youngsters prodding and poking him. Any animal would be hard pressed not to become annoyed by such interruptions to its basic needs and would quite understandably become agitated.

The first night away from his brothers and sisters can be a traumatic time for any puppy. He will have been used to the companionship and warmth offered by his siblings, and will naturally feel quite lonely on this first night in a strange place.

Decide which room you are going to let the puppy sleep in – if it is your bedroom you most probably will not experience any problems at all, apart from the fact that he will want to share your bed! If you decide to leave you puppy in, say, the kitchen, make up a comfortable bed so that he will be warm and relaxed, well out of any draughts, and then settle him down for the night with some of his favourite biscuits as a 'nightcap'. You may hear a few heartfelt cries initially, but he should settle down eventually to a good night's sleep. The gentle ticking of a clock, or music playing quietly from a radio can alleviate some of the young puppy's concern at being away from his family this first night.

There are many beds on the market, from wicker ones to heavy-duty plastic ones, to bean bags. As your puppy's teeth begin to change, he will more than likely have a tendency to chew and because of this I would advise against a wicker bed. When chewed, these can become quite sharp and could cause a cut in your dog's mouth or maybe even your leg, should you accidently brush against it. Your Dane should live with you in your house, as one Great Dane should never be confined to living on his own in a kennel. I have several dogs living with

Noah Le Mare – infant and puppies.

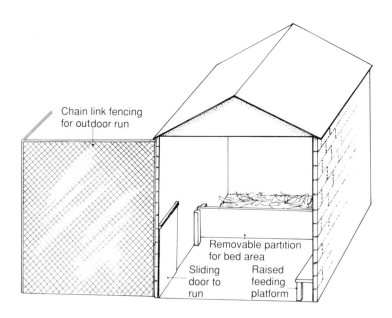

Outdoor kennel showing access to run.

me indoors, including at the moment two Great Danes, a Doberman, a Miniature Pinscher and a Chihuahua – plus several cats!

Being a breeder of Great Danes, for obvious reasons they are kennelled outside. I always run two Danes together, usually a male and a female. They have kennel areas that house ample sleeping quarters. In one corner they have a raised platform for their feeding bowls, an area with a removable partition where they sleep and a sliding door leading out into their run. These kennels are well insulated with plenty of warm bedding. Their outside runs measure approximately 50 × 8ft (15 × 2.5m) each and here they can run in the daytime. In the centre is a raised platform where they love to lie and survey everything that is going on around them. As well as having the freedom of this area, they are also exercised on a regular basis to keep them in the peak of condition.

Early Training

As the new owner of a young Dane puppy, you need to be one step ahead of his thinking. No longer can you leave your new pair of best leather shoes lying idly around as there will be nothing more tempting to a puppy than these. You cannot really blame him for not being able to tell the difference between these and perhaps those chewy toys that you give him.

It is important to teach your puppy in these early days not to clamber on to your three-piece suite! There is no need to become too heavy-handed about this, as a firm 'Down' or 'No' will dissuade him from doing it, but it is important to ensure that your puppy understands what is required of him when you give him commands. After all, he only wants a little home comfort – unfortunately, though, there will be little room for anyone else should your Dane permanently claim this as 'his seat'. If space permits you may let your Dane puppy become used to a special chair or small couch especially for him. This is an ideal state of affairs but make sure that he realizes that this is the only seat in the house that he can sit in. Therefore, when you tell your puppy from the beginning that this is the rule of the house, make sure that this is adhered to. Do not be tempted to turn a blind eye on the odd occasion, or be overruled by another member of the family. Make sure that you all follow this rule; conflicting ideas will only confuse your puppy and is not fair on him.

Dogs respond to the tone of your voice rather than to what you say. When you are telling your dog that he should not jump up on to the settee, the tone of the word 'No', said firmly as you push or lead him off, is what he will respond to. For instance, you could say 'Yes' in exactly the same manner and the effect would be the same. If your commands are carried out correctly and consistently your Dane will always know whether he is right or wrong. A dog needs to be able to tell the difference and will learn quickly when he does.

As with the commands that are given to ensure that your Dane does not do what you don't want him to do, always remember to be lavish with your praise when he pleases you or does something right. As time progresses, he will soon differentiate between the varying cadences of your voice and react accordingly. When you eventually attend your local training class with him (*see* page 80), this knowledge will aid both you and your dog as you go through your paces together.

Leaving a Puppy at Home

You would be surprised how many times you hear people say that they cannot leave their pet even for a short while because it hates to be on its own and, even more important, cannot be trusted on its own. As with any training of your youngster, the earlier he becomes accustomed to set routines, the easier and quicker he will learn to accept these rules as a normal sequence of events and part of his everyday life. In this particular instance, it is best to start this part of his training as early as possible.

If you have decided that your puppy should be trained to sleep in the kitchen at night, you will have taken the first step towards letting him get used to his own company. Whenever you are going to leave your puppy, always make sure that everything that could appear tempting is placed well out of reach, but leave him his own toys for him to play with. Never leave your puppy initially during the day for a long period of time.

If you are going out for a while, try to limit it to no longer than a couple of hours. This can be extended gradually so that when you are asked out for dinner one evening it will not be a traumatic experience, either for you or your dog. If you have to go out for a long time, perhaps for the day, make arrangements for a friend or neighbour to call in and let the youngster out and, if need be, feed him with the meal that you will have left prepared.

Car Journeys

The style and size of your car will influence whereabouts in it you wish your dog to sit. If it is an estate car, the rear of this is an ideal place for your puppy to learn to travel. I would suggest that a dog guard be fitted, if possible, so that your puppy will become used to being confined to that section; he will be secure and prevented from wandering around the car. To make it comfortable for him, place some bedding or perhaps a bean bag there so he will become relaxed and enjoy the experience.

A word of warning: remember always how very quickly a car can heat up on hot summer days, either in direct sunlight or on humid, cloudy days, so *never* leave your dog in the car unattended for even a short spell. Always make sure also that there is adequate ventilation when the car is in motion during any hot spell.

During the first few outings your dog may not take to the motion of the car and may be travel sick. After a while he should get used to this new form of travelling, but if it becomes a problem and he shows no signs of becoming a better traveller, a travel-sick tablet given prior to any long journey should make it a more pleasant experience. Be sure to follow the manufacturer's dosage instructions.

Authorpe Harmony Bear at eleven months.

Diet

Prior to the day that you collect your puppy, always ensure that you have everything to hand that you are going to need. Ask the breeder what sort of bowls you will need, for instance, and which vitamin additives, bonemeal, etc., are required.

A good breeder will furnish you with a clear and concise diet sheet which will last throughout puppyhood. The early development and feeding of your puppy are vital for his future well-being. Because the Great Dane is a fast-growing, large dog, he depends on a carefully worked out and well-balanced diet for his formation. When you are given this sheet, study it and talk through any points that you are unsure of with the breeder. Be prepared to adhere to this diet for these are the foods and vitamins that your puppy has been used to since he was weaned away from his mother. Any major deviation from this format could cause the puppy's tummy to be badly upset and result quite quickly in severe diarrhoea.

Everyone has their own favourite 'pet' ideas on rearing so this is why it is always best to adhere to any instructions given by the person who has bred the litter, as in this way you are less likely to upset the puppy's delicate digestion. When a new owner comes to collect a puppy from me, I always ensure that they take with them the food that the puppy has been used to receiving, such as biscuit and bone-meal.

The diet sheet that I present to each new owner is a guide by which to maintain the good start and condition that the puppy has received. Upon leaving my care at approximately eight weeks, a puppy will have been used to being fed five times a day. I recommend a breakfast consisting of a mixture of best minced beef or fish, with biscuit. The biscuit needs to be soaked – this is most important – in boiling water and allowed to cool. Added to this is a teaspoon of bonemeal, a must for ensuring that these fast-growing, massive dogs receive enough calcium to help form strong bones.

At lunchtime I recommend a cereal-based meal mixed with milk. The milk should be powdered baby's milk mixed with water, making up to approximately half to three-quarters of a pint (300–400ml). I also add to this an egg yolk together with a teaspoon of honey, plus the crunched-up eggshell, itself a natural source of calcium.

The third meal of the day consists of 8oz (225g) of best cooked mince mixed with an equal volume of soaked biscuit, not forgetting the two teaspoons of bonemeal once again. For dinner, or meal number four, it is time for another cereal and milk meal but the egg yolk, shell and honey are omitted.

For the puppy's final meal of the day, I recommend a good all-in-one food, but it is very important that it is one that is not too high in protein. Too much protein can cause overheating of the bloodstream and will cause your puppy to scratch; this will bring up heatspots on the skin which can become very sore and inflamed.

The method of feeding you choose is very important for the comfort of your Dane. When you put a bowl of food on the floor in front of your puppy, stand back and watch how he eats and the way he has to stand in order to reach the bowl. You will find that he contorts his body and splays his front legs so as to get into a position to be able to eat comfortably from the bowl. Can you imagine trying to eat like this? How much better, then, to make matters a little simpler for him by raising the bowl to a convenient height.

I feed my Danes from a raised feeding bowl which can be extended to match their growth. I believe that it is far better for the dog's comfort to be able to have easy access to the bowl and better from the skeletal and conformation point of view also. If you have decided that you

Raised feeding stool.

may have the occasional litter, you would be advised to invest in such an apparatus. However, to save you any further expense at this time, a small footstool would provide an ideal 'table' for your Dane's bowl, or some telephone directories could be used. As the puppy grows, the footstool or books can be exchanged for a kitchen chair, and so forth.

House-Training

Great Danes are intelligent dogs and they learn very quickly, so house-training should not present too much of a problem, especially if some training has been started by the breeder before you pick your puppy up.

I start my puppies' house-training when they are still all in the nest together. They have a sleeping area where they can all curl up together in warmth and comfort. In front of this puppy kennel a large area is covered with newspaper with a door directly out into their run. This door is left open on fine days when they have the opportunity to go out. On wet, cold days, however, the door is kept shut and they learn to use the paper laid down for them, therefore ensuring that their bed is always kept clean and dry. This method can be applied in the house, and I would suggest that, for the first few days, newspaper is laid down on the floor in the room that you intend the dog to stay in when you are not there.

One of the easiest ways to train a dog to go to the toilet outside, is to watch over him while he eats and then, once he has done this, take him out into the garden and wait until he has done all that is required. Be sure to tell him what a good dog he is, for the more praise he receives the quicker he will realize what is correct. During these early days try not to scold him when he has an 'accident' for no doubt he will learn soon enough that outside is the place to do all this. After a few days the newspaper can be reduced, and positioned near the exit to your garden, just in case he gets caught short and cannot get your attention.

I would suggest that in these first few days you keep the puppy in this one area when you are not with him. Try not to let him have *'carte blanche'* to go where he likes throughout the house without supervision, for puppies will be puppies and a house full of exciting things can be as intriguing to a puppy as a toyshop is to children.

When your youngster has become accustomed to answering the call of nature outside, and there is no longer any need for newspapers on the floor, do not be tempted to relax your routine. Remember to regulate the times you let your Dane out to the toilet, especially just after a meal.

If an accident should occur in the house (after his early puppy days in the kitchen and the use of paper), tell him firmly 'No' and lead him outside. If then he 'asks to go out', perhaps by constantly going to the door that leads outside, when he has relieved himself be quick with your praise and he will soon learn the difference. Never be tempted to 'rub his nose in it' when he has had an accident. It is unkind and totally ineffective.

House-training is really a matter of common sense. If for some reason you have to be out of the house for a long period of time, try to ensure that someone can call in and check on your youngster, letting him out if necessary. If you always think ahead with your dog, a lifetime of enjoyment and harmony will be ensured.

Inoculations

When you collect your puppy you will need to know whether he has received any inoculations. Dogs need to be inoculated against the following major canine diseases: hardpad, distemper, leptospirosis and parvovirus. These are all described in Chapter 9.

Ch. Octavia of Helmlake.

My vet inoculates from approximately twelve weeks for the first injection, with the puppy receiving the second half two weeks later. It appears that views vary on this; some vets will give the first half at ten weeks as long as the second half is given at over twelve weeks. I have also heard of an injection that can be given to younger puppies (i.e. over six weeks), a measles vaccine which provides cover for that in-between period.

If you are picking your puppy up before he has undergone his course of immunization, you must bear in mind that this young puppy is vulnerable to these diseases that lie in wait for him in the outside world. Any puppy receives a certain amount of immunity from his mother, which carries him through the first four to six weeks. The earliest my vet will give first vaccinations is eight to ten weeks and the second at twelve weeks. This leaves two weeks, at least, when the puppy has no protection. There is no effective answer to this danger period at this time. This is why I never allow potential buyers, or any other stranger for that matter, anywhere near my very young puppies. Puppies cannot be vaccinated sooner because the antibodies provided by the mother would rapidly neutralize the vaccine. When the first vaccination is given, the immune system is stimulated but the remaining antibodies will still try to interfere therefore not giving 100 per cent protection. By twelve weeks all the antibodies will have left the puppies and the final vaccination will give full protection.

When you collect a young puppy you must always go straight home with him. Do not be tempted to stop off at a friend's house (especially if they have a dog) or stop in the street to show him to all and sundry. By doing this your puppy could easily pick up a virus to which he will have no resistance.

If your puppy is a little older and has had the first of his two injections when you collect him from the breeder, he will be just as vulnerable as if he had not been inoculated at all. The safe period does not start until two weeks after the second injection, and it is only then that you should allow your puppy out anywhere to socialize with other dogs under your supervision. This is why it is so important that a safe garden or area is available away from strange dogs, where your puppy is able to play and relieve himself.

When you take your puppy to the vet for his first course of injections, remember that there may be animals in the waiting-room with infectious illnesses. Therefore, if at all possible, I would suggest that you take your puppy down to the surgery in a car, with someone to help you. Leave your friend in the car with the puppy so that he doesn't get agitated, and go in and register yourself with the nurse. When your name is called to go in to see the vet, quickly go out and get the puppy from the car, taking him straight into the surgery. Ensure that you carry the puppy all the time, never letting him down on the ground, either in or out of the vet's surgery.

When you need to go back for the second course, remember that he will have only limited immunity. You may carry him into the waiting room, but on no account let him sniff or go up to any animals in this room; this is one of the fastest ways of contracting any virus.

Insurance

It is always advisable to insure your dog. I believe some house insur-

Ch. Danemoor the Persian Boy. (Photo: Pearce.)

ances can be arranged to include third-party cover for your dog, should he cause an accident or perhaps dig up next door's prize begonias! There are also several highly reputable firms that specialize in cover for animals of every species. With these companies your Great Dane can be insured for most things, including veterinary fees (especially useful should your Dane, for some unforeseen reason, need surgery or a long period of treatment and drugs) and covering your dog for any damage to another person or their property.

Exercise

You may be surprised to read that just a little gentle exercise is required early on, for many people assume that a Dane puppy will need to be walked a number of miles each day. This would, in fact, do far more

Taurus Summer Cloud.

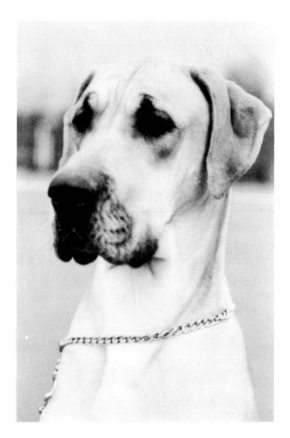

harm than good and would severely damage the development of your young dog. As I have already said, a good, balanced diet, plenty of rest and some gentle ambling are the ideal ingredients for your growing Dane. These exercise periods can be extended from perhaps a gentle walk up the road to one a little further afield once the puppy is over six months old. You have to try to keep a balance between the dog's growth and all the wonderful nutrition you are putting into him without removing it all with over-exercising.

Collar and Lead

When the puppy has settled down after a few days, I would suggest that you start to teach him to wear a collar. At first he may take complete exception to it, so for the first few days I would advise that it is left on for an hour or so only, extending this time over the following days. This can all be done in your home before the puppy starts his course of injections.

When he seems to be quite happy with his new attire and wears it quite unconsciously, start to practise with the lead as well. Again, this can be done in the home and garden without even having to take the puppy out on to the street. If this training is done early on, when the time eventually comes that you are able to take him on his first outing, he will have become used to both collar and lead.

If you are not sure what sort of collar to buy for your puppy, the breeder will be able to guide you in this matter. I recommend a good-quality leather collar for everyday use. Obviously, as your Dane grows, the notches of the collar will need to be checked regularly to make sure that it is not too tight and causing him discomfort. As the puppy grows up and outgrows his first collar, it will need to be replaced by a larger one.

If lead-training is tackled patiently and calmly, the experience can prove to be less traumatic for all concerned. It is often a good idea to let the puppy become accustomed to the lead prior to your picking up the other end. When you clip the lead on to the collar, let your Dane become used to it by allowing him to drag it about. If you are worried about the puppy chewing his new lead, tie a long piece of rope to the collar instead until he has got over this stage. Always make sure that this exercise is carried out only when you are at hand in case he should accidentally become caught around something, either frightening himself or, far worse, strangling himself.

When the puppy has become used to this latest stage of his training and his new apparel, take the end of the lead in your hand and follow him wherever he wants to go, letting him feel gentle contact with you. After a few days, when he seems to accept that you are both 'attached', gently – without yanking the lead – try to get him to start to go in the direction that you wish to take him. At this stage of the proceedings it becomes a game of give and take, and you will find that your puppy will walk with you for a certain distance, and then most likely decide to go the opposite way. Follow him for a short time, talking to him and then gently persuade him to follow you once more, always calling his name and talking to him.

If he promptly digs his heels in and refuses to budge, do not start to become involved in a tug-of-war with him; this will only serve to make matters worse. Keep the lead firmly in your hand and close the distance between you. Make a fuss of him and when you feel that he has started to relax, attempt to start off again in the direction you wish to

*Ch. Wykendrift
Marcellus.*

go, always being sure to let him know you are there. When he has obeyed your wishes, don't be tempted to overdo matters. Always end your training on a good note, letting him have a scamper off the lead around the garden, if you have been practising there. Eventually your care, kindness and patience will pay dividends and your young puppy will be quite happy to trot along by your side, ready for a life-time of enjoyable walks.

When your puppy has had all his injections and the 'safe' period of home quarantine is completed, you will then be free to take your youngster out for his first walk along the road. This will of course be yet again another 'first' for your puppy. Make quite sure that you are holding the lead firmly in your hand. Never be tempted to let one of your children hold the lead unless aided by you. If your puppy should take fright at the traffic your child would never be able to hold on to

Ch. Impton Motile.

him, and an accident could easily occur. He is about to encounter things he has never seen before: cars, bicycles, strange people, prams, other dogs and perhaps cats. If you have not got your puppy firmly under your control any one of these things could cause him to slip out of your grasp.

While on this subject, *never* be tempted to walk along the road with your dog off the lead, even when he has grown up into a fully matured adult. You can never guarantee that on seeing something interesting on the other side of the road, he would not run straight across to it.

Having become used to his short walks, from about six to eight months of age these little strolls can be extended to perhaps a walk to the park or your local common or heath. Parks and commons are breeding grounds for other dogs' germs, but you will of course have the peace of mind that your dog has been immunized against any of the major canine diseases. Nevertheless, try to dissuade him from sniffing any other dogs' faeces, as not all dogs have caring owners. Their dog may be a carrier of some virus or complaint, so try to be vigilant without becoming paranoid and spoiling these outings for both of you. Because of the problem this presents one should always keep the inoculations 'boostered', as advised by your vet.

In these early months your puppy will have only just become accustomed to walking on the lead with you and will still be inquisitive, wilful and occasionally deaf to your commands, so never be tempted to let him off the lead in the park or any open space until he is much older and more settled and you feel in control. An over-exuberant puppy will see no danger and may be carried away by the excitement of encountering other dogs; they will all think it marvellous to go galloping around the park, and possibly head for the open road.

You can allow your puppy a certain amount of leeway by using a strong extending lead, which can be purchased from most pet shops and some vets. This is an ideal way of allowing your puppy a little extra controlled freedom.

Being the owner of a dog means that you owe a certain responsibility to society as well as to the animal itself. Always remember that not everyone is equally dog orientated and there has been a lot of bad press in recent years regarding soiling in public places. Therefore, whenever you are out on a walk and your dog needs to go to the toilet, always ensure that he never does so anywhere on a public walkway. Depending on the traffic, and not putting your dog's life at risk, try to get him to do so on the side of the road or, if this is not possible, near the side of the pavement. In either case, always have a small scoop and plastic bag with you in which the faeces can then be deposited, sealed and put in the nearest litter receptacle.

There can be nothing nicer for a dog, when released from the confines of a lead, to go off at a mad gallop. Because of this, when you feel that the time has come when your dog has matured enough and is sufficiently trained to be trusted off the the lead, take him to a quiet area of the park or common well away from the road. Only do this when you are confident that he will obey you and come straight back when called. As I have said, not everyone shares your love of dogs, especially large ones. When they are confronted with 200 pounds of dog hurtling towards them, it could prove more than a little nerve-wracking for them, especially if the dog barks a greeting.

Training

By being the owner of such a beautiful, wonderful and powerful dog,

Vanmore Something Special.

you immediately owe a responsibility not only to the dog, but also to the breed of which you are an admirer and to the whole of the canine world. You must try to promote harmony between dogdom and the ordinary person in your own small way. Perhaps if everyone felt the same, a few of the anti-dog brigade would come to understand these lovely animals better.

For instance, a small dog, or Dane puppy that jumps up to meet his master can be very appealing and flattering to the receiver of such affections. Visualize, though, the same action in a fully grown adult and suddenly you are presented with the picture of a very large and powerful dog throwing his full weight. You may still be able to cope with your exuberant companion, but what would happen if the same was done to small child, an elderly or frail person or perhaps someone who was pregnant? An accident may occur that could so easily have been avoided by simple training.

How much nicer it is for someone who is a little wary of dogs, probably just because he or she has never had any association with them, to be introduced to a Dane, or any dog, by the owner of a well-behaved puppy or a calm and obedient adult.

How does one train a Great Dane to become the type of dog that will integrate easily into society? It is not a difficult task provided that you are patient and firm and keep the lessons and commands to a routine in order that the dog does not become confused.

When your puppy attempts to jump up at you and, in the process, wrap his front legs around your shoulders, use the word 'Down' forcefully. If he starts to jump up, telling him 'Down' with the palm flattened in a downward motion is effective, or 'No' with the same intonation and gesture. It is equally important to remember to praise him when he has done something that has pleased you, without getting him too excited. Pat him and stroke him, telling him all the time what a good dog he has been, and he will learn as time goes by the difference between both voices and reactions.

Training Classes

I always recommend that the new owners of any young puppy enquire in their own area about any good training classes where they and their young charge can both go for advice and group training. Very often these will be advertised in a local paper, or maybe your vet's waiting-room, or the breeder of your puppy may have some connections. Training clubs and classes are ideal places to teach your puppy all the basic commands and, equally important, help them become accustomed to being with other dogs of varying shapes and sizes, and to strangers. They will soon become used to different people handling them, pretending to judge them and generally making a fuss of them.

The majority of training clubs are split into two sections. There are those that hold classes for show training and general training while others tend to specialize in agility and general obedience training. Some others, however, may combine the two, holding separate classes on the same evening depending on the size and membership of the club itself. I would advise that initially you start your puppy at the former type of classes. Their basic aim is to teach you how to control your dog and they also incorporate show training for the would-be exhibitor and their prospective show dogs (*see* page 109). If you do not intend to show, do not be deterred, for these lessons provide very good training for any dog.

Grooming aids.

Training classes for the obedience-orientated dogs and owners teach you how to get your dog to stay, to retrieve, to walk to heel and sit on command from a distance, among other things. Danes being extremely clever dogs, easily take to this and thoroughly enjoy themselves in the process.

Grooming

A short-coated breed does not need the coat care of, say, an Old English Sheepdog, but frequent brushing is vital to encourage its healthy growth and appearance. This task need only take a few minutes each day with a body brush, as illustrated above. Regular brushing stimulates the circulation and is good for both the dog's coat and skin.

Nails

Always keep an eye on your puppy's nails for they should never be allowed to become too long. When your Dane is older, doing a lot of

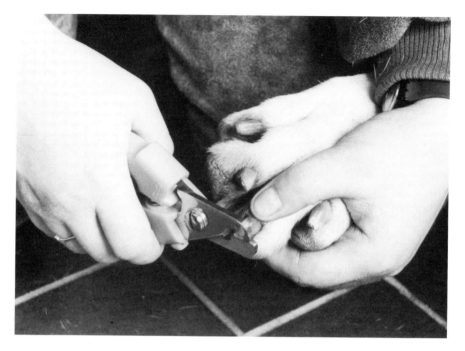

Cutting the nails.

road work will keep them down to a manageable length. When the puppy is spending time only in the house and garden you will be surprised how quickly his nails grow.

Clipping and caring for your Dane's nails can be done by you, and your puppy should become used to this routine at a young age, so that when he becomes an adult this part of his grooming will not cause too much concern. Some people feel that they can never undertake this task for the simple reason that they are frightened of making the nails bleed or hurting the dog. The breeder of the puppy will be more than pleased to show you how to do this and advise you on purchasing the necessary equipment. Your vet will also be able to assist you. With young puppies, especially those destined for the show ring, it is imperative that the nails are kept short and clean.

The Breed Standard calls for the nails of a Dane preferably to be black. This does not make the task of learning to cut them any easier for a novice. Light-coloured nails have the added advantage of revealing where the blood vessel runs; when viewing a nail from the side you will see the line running down towards the tip. This will not go as far as the end of the nail so, in order not to make the nail bleed or cause discomfort to the dog, it must be cut beyond that point.

If you cut a nail and it does bleed, don't panic. Before you tackle this part of your pet's toilet always ensure that you have at hand some potassium permanganate or a proprietary formula for stopping bleeding; when dabbed on to the nail, either of these will stop the bleeding quickly.

To cut your dog's nails you need at least two people, one to do the trimming and the other to assist in holding the dog. A Dane's leg can become quite heavy when trying to hold it and keep a check on the dog, should you try to do this on your own. If the dog moved at the crucial moment you would most likely cut in the wrong place, so make sure that you always have assistance.

Ears

It is a very important point always to keep a close check on your dog's ears or, to be more specific, the inside of the ear itself. Any continued scratching in this area or excessive shaking of the head is a sure sign that an irritation has set in, either through a build-up of wax or ear mites. If you lift up the flap of the ear and see a dark waxy substance within the ear, it needs to be cleaned out with the aid of cotton wool and ear cleanser.

There are several good ear-cleansing solutions on the market, that your breeder or your veterinary surgeon will recommend. Place a little of the solution on the cotton wool, wiping around the outer extremities of the ear. Always remember to use a different piece of cotton wool for each ear to stop the risk of spreading any infection. Next, place some of the cleanser in the ear itself, massaging the ear from the outside to allow the solution to work its way all around the inside of the dog's ear. Taking a cotton wool bud in your hand and, pulling the ear flap back with the other, very gently lift any excess wax and solution from the ear. Do not be tempted to push and prod too far down into the ear for you will inflict considerable pain and could do untold damage to the ear drum should you be too vigorous in this action. Finally wipe away any excess of wax with a piece of cotton wool.

If after a couple of days the condition has not improved, in all probability the dog has ear mites, and your Dane will need to have drops prescribed by a vet to help clear this up. The vet will most probably take a scraping of the substance from inside the ear itself and analyse it to find out what is causing the irritation. In the early stages it is not a serious condition, but if left untreated and unattended it could very

Ch. Campeador de los Mandronales of Helmlake.

well turn into something that may need more intensive treatment and, in very bad cases, surgery on the ear.

Bathing

How often should you bath a Dane? The simplest answer to this is, as often as you feel it is needed. However, with regular grooming and care of your dog's skin and coat this should not need to be carried out too often. It is always advisable, though, to let your Great Dane become used to being bathed from a reasonably early age, for your benefit as well as his.

In the summer it is much easier to bath your Dane on a hot day, when he can be towel-dried and left. In winter, in the average house, it causes more problems. If you wash your Dane in the bath, ensure you have a strong rubber non-slip mat in place to prevent him from slipping. It will give him more confidence if his feet can grip something firm.

You have a wide choice of shampoos and if you are going to bath your Dane occasionally, an insecticidal one would be advisable. If you are bathing him to go to a show, there are also some very good coat-conditioning shampoos on the market.

Always ensure that you have removed all the soap from the dog's coat in the final rinse before drying him off, for this could easily set up an irritation to the skin. Always try to keep the soap out of his eyes, especially an insecticidal one, and ensure that you keep his ears as dry as possible, for if water gets inside the ear, it may cause problems.

The Elderly Dane

As your Dane grows older he will become very much an integrated part of your life giving you a lot of joy, love and wonderful memories. Unfortunately, the average life-span of a dog is but a fraction of ours and as he becomes older, as with anyone of advancing years, the body and its workings begin to suffer from fatigue and becomes worn out.

Therefore, do not scold your elderly dog if an accident occurs in an otherwise house-trained dog because he could not manage to reach the garden in time. Learn to adapt your routine and let him out for his exercise more frequently. In bad weather especially, try not to leave him outside for more than a short time and if the weather is wet or snowy, make sure that you dry him off as soon as he comes indoors. Always check that he does not lie in any draughts and let him sleep undisturbed and unbothered by other animals or children.

Old age comes to us all, so make sure that you make your dog's twilight years as comfortable as you possibly can. If the time is near for you to have to make that fateful decision to say a final farewell to your friend, however heartbreaking it will be, remember you owe it to him to make his end as peaceful and dignified as possible. You owe him that for a lifetime of devotion and love that you both shared.

5

Showing

In my experience the majority of showgoers are those who primarily bought a Great Dane merely as a pet and companion and then for some reason discovered an urge to show their dog competitively. Very often this comes about when a puppy has been sold as a pet and then blossoms from what was a nice animal into something even more promising than could originally have been predicted. If a breeder adheres to the system that I insist on – of asking you to bring the young Dane back to him regularly for monitoring – you will then get an expert opinion on his show potential.

Many owners have no desire whatsoever to involve themselves in the world of showing and their dog to them will, in their eyes, always be a 'Crufts Champion' even if he never sees the inside of a show ring. But there are those who become totally fascinated by the thought of showing and all that it involves. If you wish to embark on this hobby and are willing to accept all the various ups and downs that accompany it, you will find an endless involvement and fascination for as long as you care to be active in this field. But if you are looking for a way of bolstering up your own self-esteem through the hoped for successes of your Dane, you will find it to be a rather empty hobby. As with any hobby or way of life, you will only get back out of it what you are prepared to put in.

Another important point is – can you take it when your pride and joy is not placed, when in your eyes he is equally as beautiful as the winner? Can you take it when you have travelled miles and miles only to be unplaced at a show after having perhaps done very well at one the week before? Can you take the good with the bad, the rough times with the smooth? This is all part and parcel of dog showing. If the answer is 'no' then it is best now to dispense altogether with the idea of showing.

You must try to keep everything in perspective. However much you want to win and think that your dog is good enough to win, sometimes things may not quite go as well as you would wish them to. You

Ch. Imperial Measure of Helmlake. (Photo: Pearce.)

must try to disregard the negative side and not feel that you have been badly done by; you should certainly not bore everyone in sight by recounting your feelings to them. Unfortunately not everyone can win every time; it has to be accepted that on one day you may have a very good show, while the next excursion might not be so successful. Taken in the right spirit, dog showing can be a very enjoyable pastime providing you don't let the very few 'moaners', who for various reasons constantly fail to have success in the ring, infect you with their depressing utterances.

One of the main points to remember when showing your dog is that win or lose, your Great Dane is no lesser an animal if he fails to win that esteemed first prize. Your dog will love you just as much when he returns home without a prize card as he did when you left home that morning. Don't let him down by not reciprocating his love and devotion.

Having decided to show your dog, the first thing to do is familiarize yourself with the various types of show and the way the show system works.

Ch. Mahe of Helmlake. (Photo: Pearce.)

Types of Show

These fall into four categories: Exemption Shows, Limited Shows, Open Shows and Championship Shows. The last three can also be separated into two types, the All Breed and Breed Club Shows. These shows can be found advertised in the canine press, *Our Dogs* or *Dog World*. You will probably also see them advertised in your local paper or possibly your vet's surgery and pet shop.

All Breed Shows and Breed Club Shows

These are defined as they sound. An All Breed Show is where dogs of various breeds compete together. They will offer classes for particular breeds, for example classes for Great Danes, German Shepherds, etc. These may change from show to show for it is dependent on each society and show committee which breeds are designated their own classes. There will also be on offer Variety classes and these in turn are segregated into Any Variety Not Separately Classified and Variety classes. The difference between these is that the former, or in its widely accepted abbreviated form AVNSC, is only for dogs not given classes of their own, whereas in Variety classes a dog can be entered in one or more of these classes after having been entered in classes specifically defined for his breed.

If you are fortunate enough to be made Best AVNSC Puppy or Best AVNSC, you will be eligible to compete at the end of the day for Best in Show. Winners of classes, however, are not permitted to compete in the finals.

A Breed Club Show is confined to dogs of one particular breed. Unlike the All Breed Open Shows, the classification is both generous and widespread. There are usually on average only four classes on offer for the Breed at an All Breed Show whereas at a Breed Club Show there can be as many as twenty plus. There are classes for both sexes right through from Minor Puppy to the Open class .

Exemption Shows

This type of show is one for show dogs and family pets alike. There are usually several classes for pedigree dogs; combined with these are classes that are perhaps a little less sophisticated but great fun. There are sometimes classes for the 'Dog With The Waggiest Tail' and 'The Dog That Looks Most Like His/Her Owner', which can provide endless amusement to all concerned.

Exemption Shows are usually very well supported and you will see many young up-and-coming show dogs smoothing off a few rough edges on these days. These shows, accompanied by the classes offered at training, are ideal as first shows for your dog for they give both you and your charge a chance to practise ring procedure and to gain confidence ready for the 'Big Day'. You would obviously be best advised to enter the pedigree classes rather than the novelty classes alone. However, if you want a bit of fun and provided that your puppy is not tired or overcome by the event, the novelty classes can provide a little light-hearted diversion for you both.

Limited Shows

Limited Shows are those limited usually to dogs that are not Champions, or alternatively the show may be limited to members only. Limited Shows can be either All Breed or Breed Club Shows.

Daneways Dolly Clothes Peg.

Ch. Batsworth Obsession at Marridane. (Photo: Pearce.)

Open Shows

Open Shows are the opposite to Limited Shows in that they do allow Champions to be shown; there is no restriction on this. Again, these can be either All Breed or Breed Club Shows, where both can attract very stiff and keen competition.

Championship Shows

The ultimate in dog shows, these are the only shows where a dog can gain the Challenge Certificates needed to enable him to become a Champion. As with the previously mentioned shows, they are once again split into two denominations – Breed Club and All Breed Shows. At both of these, the Kennel Club allow their Challenge Certificates (CCs) to be awarded. The Kennel Club allot a set number of CCs, also known as 'tickets', to be awarded each year, and this varies depending on the breed; therefore even though it is an All Breed Championship Show, one should always check the classification to see if CCs are

Ch. Dicarl the Lioness of Jafrak. (Photo: Pearce.)

available there. It should be noted that just because classes are scheduled, it does not necessarily mean that Championship status is attached to them. The classes are judged in the same manner with a Best of Breed being chosen at the end. At All Breed Championship Shows, the Best of Breed winner is still entitled to enter in the class for Best in Show along with the others, even when there are no CCs to be handed out.

At a Championship Show two sets of Challenge Certificates can be offered, one for each sex. A Great Dane, as with any other breed, needs three CCs to become a Champion, and these must have been won under three different judges. The dog must also be over twelve months of age when receiving the third CC. With each Challenge Certificate that is handed out comes a Reserve Challenge Certificate. These are awarded to exhibits in both sexes that are, in the judge's mind, worthy of being awarded a CC should the winner be disqualified for some reason.

Crufts

Started originally by Charles Cruft, this show has gone from strength to strength, and has just celebrated its hundredth birthday. Up until 1991 the qualification for entry had become more and more strict (you have to qualify to go there; unlike other shows, you are unable just to enter). It was, until recently, only the winners (first place) of Puppy, Junior, Post Graduate, Limit and Open that were able to compete at this show of shows. Crufts up until 1991 had always been staged in London, its last venue there being Earls Court, but, owing to space being at a premium, provision had to be made to prevent overcrowding, which was one of the reasons for the restrictions. The National Exhibition Centre at Birmingham, however, is now the venue and, as this has more space and can cater for the extra dogs, the qualifier was relaxed in the year preceding the centenary show. The first three places in the Puppy classes, Junior classes, Post Graduate, Limit and Open were able to enter at Crufts 1991.

Choosing a Show

When you are looking for a show to attend, I would advise that you start at the beginning and choose a Limited or an Open Show. Visit a few first, as a spectator, and watch the exhibitors with their dogs. See how they handle them; you will soon be able to spot the true

Ch. and Int. Ch. Airways Wrangler of Impton.

professional, the handler who can make his dog look 'just right' at the all-important moment when the judge's eyes are looking for the winner. The handler who manages to make the dog stand correctly and at the same time get that little bit extra out of him at precisely the right moment, with hardly any visible effort, is a delight to watch.

You will also be able to see those in the ring who are more interested in what is going on out of the ring than in what is actually happening in it. And there will be those who are perhaps a little too flamboyant, taking away the desired statuesqueness of their magnificent dog. The art of good handling is to have your dog looking well groomed, happy and alert while standing to perfection, presenting the picture of the desired Great Dane, while you melt into the background. Watch the exhibitors going through their paces. This is where hopefully you should see how a triangle is performed to perfection by the experienced. You will see immediately those in tune with their dogs. It almost seems to appear as an invisible thread where dog and handler are linked, giving and receiving the right responses from each other. This does not just happen; it has to be worked at and practised with patience and kindness.

When you have satisfied yourself that both you and your Great Dane are ready for your first excursion into the show world, you need to find a show that is reasonably close to home for this first outing. An Exemption Show is usually the best, and will not be too nerve-wracking an experience for either of you. At an Exemption Show, entries are taken on the day of the show only, so as soon as you arrive you will need to give the show manager details of your dog and the classes in which you wish to enter.

If you have decided to make an Open or Limited Show the place for you both to make your début, I would suggest on this first occasion that you do not venture too far afield. Your young dog will feel more at ease with a short journey than one lasting two hours or so, especially if he is not a wonderful traveller in these early days.

You will soon come to learn that your dog will know whenever there is a 'show in the air'. Why that should be one will never know, perhaps it is because of the preparation of your show bag, etc., or perhaps the signals you are exuding.

Further details of the shows advertised in the dog papers can be received by ringing the secretary or show manager (whichever num-

Yacanto I'm Mandy. (Photo: Pearce.)

ber is quoted) and a schedule can also be obtained from them. An advertisement will give you the date of the show together with the closing date. The closing date is the last date on which your letter can be posted, and will be the last acceptable time your entry can be accepted by its postmark. Allow plenty of time for the society to post your schedule to you so that your entries can be sent back as quickly as possible.

Classes

When you receive your schedule, study it carefully to decide which class your Dane should be entered in. A young puppy is able to go into the Minor Puppy or Puppy class. The Minor Puppy class is for puppies from six to nine months of age, while the Puppy class is for those up to twelve months.

At an All Breed Open Show there are always four classes on offer for the breed and will be for both sexes. At a Breed Club Open Show you will find that the classes are segregated for dogs and bitches and will be greater in number.

An All Breed Open Show usually carries the following classes: Puppy, Novice, Graduate or Postgraduate, and Open.

With a young puppy it is best to limit yourself to the Puppy class alone, although, depending on how mature he is, you may wish to enter him for the Novice class. You may also decide to enter one of the Variety classes for a little extra experience. Do not be tempted to enter each and every class in your breed with your youngster. A puppy will be hard pressed to come out on top in a strong Open class which, in most cases, will contain many much more mature dogs, including dogs of probably two or more years that have been winning fairly regularly.

Novice is for dogs that have not won a Challenge Certificate or three more prizes at Open or Championship Shows (Minor Puppy, Special Minor Puppy, Puppy, Special Puppy classes excepted, whether restricted or not).

Graduate is for dogs that have not won a Challenge Certificate or four or more first prizes at Championship Shows in Graduate, Postgraduate, Minor Limit, Mid Limit, Limit and Open classes, whether restricted or not.

Postgraduate is for dogs that have not won a Challenge Certificate or five or more first prizes at Championship Shows in Postgraduate, Minor Limit, Mid Limit, Limit and Open Classes, whether restricted or not.

Ch. Dorneywood Sebastian. (Photo: Pearce.)

Open is for all dogs of the breed for which the class is provided and eligible for entry at the show. Remember, of course, that at a Limited Show the definitions for Open will be different.

At an All Breed Championship, or Breed Club Show, whether it is Open or Championship, the classes are more varied for not only do you have a Puppy class, a Minor Puppy class will also no doubt be included. Junior is another well-attended class and at some All Breed Open Shows this is also scheduled. This is for dogs of six to not exceeding eighteen months of age on the first day of the show.

It is inadvisable to put a six-month-old puppy into a Junior class for the simple reason that he may be competing with dogs of nearly eighteen months of age. Also, these dogs may have won in very keen competition throughout their puppy career and have extended on into this class. It is always a very good class to win, especially the higher up the scale of shows you go. Special Yearling is another class that can house some top-winning animals. It is usually confined to Club Shows or Championships only, particularly the latter, and is for dogs of between twelve and twenty-four months of age.

Novice and Maiden are also classes that can be included at a Club Show. The definition of novice has already been covered, while Maiden is for dogs which have not won a Challenge Certificate or a first prize at an Open or Championship Show (Minor Puppy, Special Minor Puppy, Puppy and Special Puppy classes excepted, whether restricted or not).

Graduate and Post Graduate are offered generally at Open Club Shows and once again we have covered the definitions.

Limit is the next class and is for dogs that have not won three Challenge Certificates or seven or more first prizes in all at Championship Shows in Limit and Open Classes confined to the breed, whether restricted or not, at shows where Challenge Certificates were offered for the breed.

Open classes we have covered and the same definitions apply. This is the class where you will find the vast majority of Champions entered, if any, but of course there is nothing to stop a Champion entering in a Junior or Special Yearling class, providing the age barrier does not preclude it.

There may also be Champions in the Limit class, for they may of course have entered the show having won only two CCs and received their third and qualifying Challenge Certificate after entries had closed. At Club Shows there will also be classes scheduled for colour, with their own definitions.

At an All Breed Championship Show, the classes offered usually total fourteen approximately, whereas at a Breed Club Show, whether it be Open or Championship, there could be about twenty-four classes.

For your first couple of outings, remember to restrict yourself to the Open or Limited Shows. By starting in the 'shallow end', so to speak, you will both be learning and building up your confidence ready for the day when you take the plunge into the Championship Show arena.

This may all sound a bit dramatic, but you will find, especially after you have been showing for a little while, that there is definitely more tension and excitement generated at the shows at Championship level than those a little further down the scale. Although competition is still in evidence at the smaller shows, there is probably not the same quality and not quite so much at stake. The Championship Shows hold that little extra something, no doubt because entrants may win an honour that will make a dog a Champion.

You will have now been taking your dog regularly to his training classes and practising for a few minutes each day at home. You will

Ch. Picanbil Pericles and Ch. Arianne of Auldmoor. (Photo: Lewis.)

also have been attending some of the shows watching the various handlers in the ring. Whenever you have a problem or are merely wishing to learn, you will have been seeking your breeder's advice, whose knowledge is gleaned from years of experience. All this time you and your Dane will have been forming a very special partnership, and will eventually be ready to compete at the Open Shows before going on to the larger Championship Shows.

At an All Breed Open Show you will invariably find that only local dogs will compete against each other. A Breed Club Open Show will draw competition from further afield. Championship Shows will obviously attract dogs from all parts of the country. At these shows you

Ch. Devarro Governor's Envoy of Gazabbie. (Photo: Dalton.)

will see the same dogs, many of them consistent winners on the circuits. With entry fees and travelling, this does not go towards making dog showing a cheap hobby!

The Entry Form

When you are entering your puppy at his first show you will need to have all the following details at hand: his registered name, date of birth and names of the sire and dam. With each schedule that is sent out is included an entry form for that particular show. The All Breed Championship Shows usually include two for those people showing more than one breed. However, most of the Club Shows and Open All Breed and Limited Shows allow you just one.

If the breeder has applied to the Kennel Club for the name the puppy is to be registered as, but has not received the official acceptance back, you are still able to enter the puppy but by the side of the name entered you need to put the letters 'NAF' (Name Applied For), together with 'TAF' (Transfer Applied For). If you have received the registration forms from the breeder and have in turn sent them off

99

Ch. Hotpoint's New Treasure for Batworth. (Photo: Pearce.)

yourself to the KC and are still awaiting their reply, only the letters 'TAF' need be included on the form.

Make sure that your puppy will be at least six months old on the day of the show. Whether he should be entered for the Minor Puppy or Puppy class depends on how mature he appears. If you are not sure, ask advice from your breeder or any other knowledgeable person.

Before we proceed any further I would advise you to keep a show record of your dog's wins. This can be obtained from one of the stands at a dog show and come in the form of a little booklet. This is most invaluable for working out your dog's wins; you will need to know exactly how his career has progressed when it comes to entering in such classes as Novice, Maiden, Postgraduate, Limit and Open.

The next question to be filled in is the sex of the dog, whether it is male or female. Then the breed of the dog needs to be recorded, followed by the dog's date of birth. You will next be asked for the name of

Ch. Dicarl the Lioness of Jafrak and Ch. Dicarl the Heavyweight. (Photo: Pearce.)

the breeder of your puppy. The next two columns are fairly self-explanatory, asking for the names of your puppy's parents which of course you should have from the pedigree and registration papers received from the breeder.

The final column asks for the class or classes your puppy is to be entered in. Make quite sure that you have the class numbers entered correctly, for it is very easy when you are in a rush to make a mistake and enter a baby puppy in something like Limit. Once you are at the show you are unable to transfer back to the class of your choice once the entry is recorded by the show society and is printed in the catalogue. The only transfer you are allowed to do is to go into the Open class which, of course, is hardly fair on a puppy still in his growing stages as he will have to compete against fully mature dogs. Once you have completed these sections, the next most important step is to fill in your name and address with your telephone number.

You also need to check on whether or not you will need a pass for parking your car. Some societies include this free of charge, while others make a basic charge. If it is the latter, the ticket should be included when your passes are sent out.

The All Breed Open Show, Limited Show and Club Show entry forms are all basically set out in this fashion. The All Breed Championship Show entry forms are set out in a similar fashion but are slightly more extensive. One can get severe writer's cramp after filling out the various sections! They will, for instance, expect you to fill in your name and address for next year's catalogues and your passes. It is a good idea to buy some small pre-printed labels with all your details on, which can save a great deal of time and effort.

Passes are sent out by the major All Breed Championship Shows prior to the day of the show. They will include the name of the dog and also his ring number in most cases. Owing to ever rising costs, most of the Club, All Breed Open and Limited Shows have ceased to send these out. If you require confirmation of your entry being received you will need to include with your entries a stamped self-addressed envelope requesting that this be sent to you.

When you have completed the entry form and worked out the relevant fee, always ensure that you mark on the schedule itself which classes you have entered. If in later years you are showing more than one dog, this is quite invaluable. It is not unheard of for someone to take the wrong dog to a show.

The entries need to be sent no later than the date specified on the schedule. It states which date that is and will also say 'postmark'. This means that if an envelope is received postmarked later than the specified date, the entry will not be accepted by the secretary or show manager on behalf of the society.

There is also the possibility that the Post Office may let you down by losing your letter somewhere along the way. Of course in all innocence you would arrive at the show to find that you are not even entered in the catalogue. Then follows a lot of aggravation all round while trying to sort this out and find out if you are able to show or not.

Ch. Timellie Caspian. (Photo: Pearce.)

Some societies will let you show and report this to the Kennel Club automatically, who will in turn ask you for proof that you had indeed sent off the entry. You know yourself, of course, that your entries had genuinely become lost in the GPO system somewhere along the line, but you can hardly blame the canine authority for being a little sceptical. You can prove that your entries were sent on or before the desired time that the Kennel Club will accept with a 'Proof Of Posting' slip. Any Post Office will offer this service free of charge. You simply hand your letter over the counter and they return a slip of paper to you, date stamped on the day of posting which confirms that you have posted the letter.

The Points System

Apart from the obvious delight of winning a first prize at any show, the win may mean that you will also receive Junior Warrant Points. These are given for first prize wins at either Open or Championship

Shows in classes specified for the breed. A win in a variety class of any description does not entitle you to any points at all. Up until quite recently it was decreed by the Kennel Club that Junior Warrant Points could be awarded to dogs winning first prizes at any of the specified shows provided they were between six and eighteen months of age.

A win at a Championship Show would give the recipient three points, while a similar win at an Open Show would be rewarded with one point. Provided that a dog was shown regularly, extensively and in several classes at each show attended, and that the said Dane resembled a show dog, this was not usually a difficult win to attain. Nowadays it has been made a little more difficult to win, and is therefore worth a lot more to both owner and dog. A dog must now be between twelve and eighteen months of age, thus restricting the time allowed to be able to accrue the points by six months.

Unlike a Challenge Certificate that is handed out on the day to the winning dog, the winner needs to apply to the Kennel Club on the relevant form, listing the wins and appropriate points awarded. To obtain the necessary form, you may either apply to the Kennel Club itself or, at many of the large All Breed Championship Shows, the Kennel Club have a mobile stand where the majority of forms can be obtained.

Champions

How do you make a Champion? This is something to which everyone who shows dogs aspires at some time or other. In the United Kingdom, I have already mentioned that you need three Challenge Certificates to be awarded by three different judges in order for your dog to gain the title. The Challenge Certificates are designated to the shows throughout the UK by the Kennel Club.

There are also kennel clubs in other parts of the country, for instance the Scottish Kennel Club has gone from strength to strength in recent years, offering administrative skills as well as the two major Championship Shows that they host twice a year near Edinburgh. The Welsh Kennel Club always keeps a welcome at its highly popular show which is held at Builth Wells set deep in the midst of the Welsh heartland.

The Irish Kennel Club, which covers Eire, has its own system, both of registering dogs and show awards. Dogs have to be registered with

Ch. Helmlake Quo Vadis. (Photo: Pearce.)

the Irish Kennel Club before they can be shown there. So if you live outside the area of the Irish Kennel Club, you are allowed to show your dogs there at their highly popular shows and circuits, only if you register them first with the Irish Kennel Club. In Eire the award given towards making a dog or bitch into a Champion is known as a Green Star. Each Green Star is worth a certain number of points and these are dependent on the dogs entered and actually present on the day. If the entry was numerically strong on the day, the Green Star awarded may be worth five points, whereas in a mediocre entry it would be worth much less. Therefore, absenteeism is very important in this system for this may mean the difference of some very important points towards a Championship. The total number of points needed to warrant the title of Champion is fifteen. As with the Reserve Challenge Certificates awarded under the UK system, a Reserve Green Star is also handed out as a safeguard against possible disqualification of the winner.

In the United States another system is in operation. In most ways it is similar to that operated by the Irish kennel Club, being also dependent on a points system. Their awards are known as Winners Dog and Winners Bitch, again with Reserves being available.

In the United States, a dog is allowed to be entered in only one class. When the judging is completed, all the unbeaten dogs are called into the ring and are judged for the award of Winners Dog or Winners Bitch, with the appropriate Reserves. When both sexes have been judged and the awards given, both the Winners Dog and Winners Bitch come back into the ring to compete for Best of Winners.

With the American system, unlike that in operation in the UK, Champions are not allowed to compete in the regular classes. They make their appearance only after both Winners awards have been handed out. It is then that the Champions class is called into the ring. All those Champions present, together with the Best of Winners, then compete for Best of Breed. Each Champion is assessed individually and judged as any class would be judged.

In the UK, any one dog is able to go in as many classes as the owner chooses to enter. However, to compete for the Challenge Certificate only unbeaten dogs are allowed to be present in the ring, i.e. dogs that have not been beaten by any other dog on that particular day.

When your dog is young and learning and you want to give him as much practice as possible, it is a good idea to enter a few classes. When the time comes and he has matured and is perhaps reaching an age where if he wins a class he may be considered for something higher, I would advise that you restrict yourself always to just one class.

Best of Breed and Show

Similar to the American system, in the UK the Dog CC challenges the Bitch CC winner for Best of Breed. If the show is a Club Show with just one breed scheduled, this award is known as Best in Show. If it is an All Breed Show, the Best of Breed, as it will then be known, competes against others from its group for Best in Group. The final consists of all the group winners then coming together to see which dog will win the Best in Show award.

Dogdom segregates its various breeds into a selection of groups. In the UK, for instance, there are six: the Working Group (numerically the largest of the groups), into which the Great Dane falls, the Hound Group, the Utility Group, Gundog Group, Toy Group and Terrier Group. In the USA these are split into seven groups: the

*Ch. Drumview Trade Secret winning the group at Blackpool
Championship Show. (Photo: Hartley.)*

Sporting Group, the Hound Group, the Working Group (once again
the group that includes the Great Dane), the Herding Group, Terrier
Group, Toy Group and Non-Sporting Group. Up until 1983 the
Working Group in the USA was, as in Great Britain, the largest of the
groups, comprising thirty-two breeds. The American Kennel Club
decided in 1982 to split this group, thus making the seventh group
which became known as the Herding Group.

An All Breed Championship Show in the United Kingdom is split
over a number of days; this can be anything from two to four days
depending on the show society. Usually the lengthier shows allow the
Working Group to be staged on a separate day from the other groups.
Therefore, when judging has been completed in all rings, all the Best of
Breeds throughout the Working Group compete against each other for
Group Winner and Reserve Group Winner. When all the Groups have
been judged and every winner picked, all the group winners then
compete with each other for Best in Show. Of course, this entails group

winners from the previous day or days having to return for the Grand Finale.

Most All Breed Open Shows in the United Kingdom confine their shows to a single day, although a few of the very large ones, especially those held in conjunction with a County or Agricultural show, will be held over two days. In the case of the latter shows, the group system is often executed and works in basically the same way as at the premier shows. The only difference in most cases is that a Best in Show for the first day would be made, so that only one dog comes back to compete against the dog chosen from the group winners on the following day.

With one-day Open Shows, either a group system is operated or all unbeaten dogs compete together in the ring where a Best in Show or Reserve Best in Show is picked from their number.

Best Puppy

I would think that in 99 per cent of cases, shows will offer a Best Puppy award within the breed, where puppy classes are scheduled. Almost without exception All Breed Open Shows offer a final for unbeaten puppies, which is staged in a similar fashion to Best in Show. Although at an All Breed Championship Show a Best Puppy will be found from within the breed, in some cases a final may not be held. It is always advisable to check in the schedule or catalogue on the day.

Puppy Stakes

This is an entirely different competition from the ordinary puppy classes within the breed or even the variety puppy classes at All Breed Open Shows. They are invariably a sponsored event and will be held over the full period of a Championship Show. The stakes classes will be scheduled to coincide with the particular groups staged on each day.

This is a separate class and should be entered as such. From the entrants on each day the first five will compete for the title of overall winner for that particular day. As with the group winners, the stakes winners are required to return for the finals of that particular heat on the last day of the show. Once an overall winner has been chosen, that dog will be invited, with other heat finalists, to compete at a prestigious competition at the end of the season's shows. As well as the

Ch. Helmlake Quo Vadis winning the Champion Stakes at Peterborough Championship Show.

Puppy Stakes competitions, there are other similar stakes classes for Champions and veterans also.

Show Training

There should be a class at your local training club which will train dogs specifically for shows. The normal pattern of events is that such a class will commence with each owner being asked to stand his dog in the show position. The person taking the class, as 'judge' for the evening, may now proceed to walk down the line of dogs. Having done this he will then start to go over each dog individually, handling him at the same time. In a variety class at an All Breed Show it is common practice for the smaller dogs, or 'table dogs', to be positioned by the ring steward at the head of the line, while the larger breeds assessed on the ground follow on.

'Table dogs' are those dogs handled by the judge on a table that is set

Brindle puppy being set up in the show pose.

in the ring for this purpose. Toy breeds, for example, are judged in this manner, as are many of the Utility Group such as the glamorous Lhasa Apso, the Shih Tzu, the Tibetan Spaniel, the Miniature and Toy Poodles. Another reason the table dogs are segregated from their larger companions is that when a judge asks the dogs to circle around the ring together, very often the smaller dogs are sent around first before the others make the same manoeuvre. This ensures that the faster-moving dogs are not impeded in their movement, or the smaller dogs alarmed by being overtaken by them.

When it is your turn for your dog to be handled by the judge you will need to move him out of line and to a position at the top of the ring near the official's table. Stand your dog in the show position ready for the judge or trainer to go over. A lot of this training can be started at home. Teach your puppy from an early age how to stand still and correctly.

Lead him around to the front of you, and make sure that he is standing with both front legs straight and firm. When he seems happy with this, ensure that his back legs are positioned so that they stretch out slightly behind him, with the hocks even with each other. The lead, preferably a show lead (as illustrated on page 114), should be up under the ears and well under the throat.

The judge will initially take a look at your puppy from the front, side and behind to get an overall impression of him. He will then start to handle him. When you are doing the groundwork at home and getting your puppy to stand, ask anyone who happens to be around to go through the paces of handling your dog in the same manner as a would-be judge. The more he becomes used to being handled in this way the less likely it is that he will become unsettled by a complete stranger doing the same thing to him in the show ring.

One of the first things the judge will want to do is see your dog's dentition. Some judges prefer to do this themselves while others may ask you to open the mouth for them rather than unsettle the dog or risk spreading anything contagious. To teach your puppy to become used to showing his teeth, gently lift the top lips with one hand while slightly pulling them back. At the same time, with your other hand gently pull down the lower lip slightly. Try to get your puppy used to this and to stand like this for a minute or so. European judges lay a great deal of importance on a dog's dentition and some judges set great store by having a Great Dane with the correct and desired bite.

The judge will then generally run his hands over the puppy before asking you to move him up and down the ring. When he has finished and you are ready to move, turn your puppy to face the direction that you wish to move in. Hold your lead firmly in your left hand and check that your puppy is 'with you' both physically and mentally, paying attention to what you are asking him to do.

At a training club a large dog such as a Great Dane is very much restricted as to movement; he is simply very often unable to get into his proper stride before it is time to turn. At a show, if you have a large ring be prepared to use it to its best advantage. Practise these moves in the park or where there is enough space to let your Dane be able to get into his correct stride. When you are in the ring always make a mental note of any undulating ground, any holes or bumps perhaps that could throw your dog out of stride.

When you are ready to move off, call your puppy's name so that he knows you are there. Communication between dog and handler is always very important either at training class or in the ring itself. It

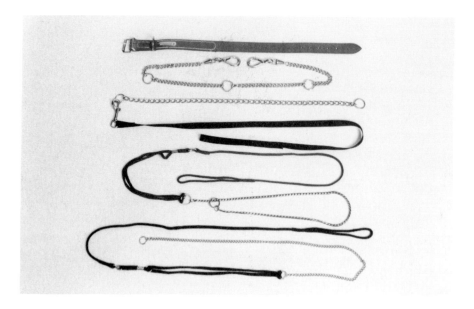

Collar, benching chain and various show leads.

helps to seal that special bond that makes it seem that dog and owner move as one. Do not feel self-conscious, for people are not interested in you making a fool of yourself, they are more interested in watching your dog and seeing how well he can move and how he shows. You will find at training classes that everyone is also only too glad to see how you both progress as the time goes on and a great deal of friendliness and camaraderie is in evidence at these events.

Your puppy will get his confidence from you and from hearing your voice so if he is feeling a little wary on the first couple of occasions, or perhaps takes complete exception to a particularly noisy or aggressive dog, talk to him to reassure him until eventually he will learn to take all these things in his stride.

Before you move off with your puppy, be sure of what the judge is asking of you both. Did he ask you to perform a triangle or just to go straight up and down, or both? You would be surprised how many people find it difficult to move in a triangle. Some exhibitors still insist on going straight up and down however many times they are asked, while it is patently obvious that some others did not score very high marks for geometry at school. To complete a triangle you need to start at a point near the judge bearing right in a straight line while going up

Setting hindquarters in the show pose.

the ring and away from the judge. Do not weave at all, just keep your dog going straight; in this way the judge is able to assess your dog's rear action. At a point approximately three-quarters of the way up the ring, bear left going straight across the ring towards the other side. The judge will then be able to watch your dog's movement from the side while assessing his overall composition on the move. At a point near the side of the ring, bear left again so that you are heading in a straight line, this time back towards the point that you started from. The judge is now able to see your dog's front action as you return to him. Keep your dog moving smoothly and evenly, making each turn gently, and keep your dog's momentum going, thus allowing him to keep in his stride.

You will then, in the majority of cases, be asked to move your dog once again, this time away from the judge and still in a straight line, turning and returning to the same spot. When you have finished this exercise make sure that your dog is standing nicely, so that when the judge takes a final look he will remember the finished picture favourably when it comes to making his final decision. When the

Harlequin puppy set up in show pose with show lead positioned.

judge has finished with you and moved on to the next exhibit, return into line following on from those who have been seen before you. Always keep an eye on how many more dogs there are to be seen while you are standing in line, always remembering the dog that was seen first. When the judge has only a few dogs left to go over, start to get your dog ready for the moment when he will look at all of the class standing in the show position.

Always be aware of the proceedings and concentrate on what is happening. Do not become involved in a long, however interesting or scandalous, conversation with a fellow exhibitor. Your dog needs to be looking right at the moment when the judge glances over.

While the class is being judged, either at training or at a show, allow your dog to relax in between the judge seeing him and the time when the class is being finally assessed. Do not keep him constantly standing 'posed', for when the time comes for him to look the part, he will have lost that edge, and will not give of his best. He will become fidgety and restless and everything will become a chore and a bore. The secret is to keep him fresh and let him enjoy every moment that you share together in the ring.

Everything that you learn at training classes can be easily transferred to the showring and, if attended regularly, they can help to give you that well-behaved and controlled dog that you desire without losing his personality and individuality.

Prior to the Show

It is always best to have a show bag that is ready to be picked up on the morning of the show with everything in it that you are going to need for your day's outing. For instance, always ensure that all your grooming aids are ready in the bag – sprays, brushes, cloths, show leads – together with your passes, if applicable, and perhaps your car park voucher.

Your passes are essential for you to gain entry with your dog into the showground. The attendant on the gate will take half of this, leaving you with a portion which you will need in order to take your dog out of the showground. This is mainly for security purposes and helps to lessen the chance of someone else removing your dog from the showground without your knowledge. So always ensure that you keep these on you at all times.

You will need to have a bowl and a large bottle of fresh water for your dog for the day. It is always advisable to take your own tap water; it is not unheard of for water from a different area to upset your dog's digestion. You will also need to have your benching chain, which is necessary to secure your Dane to the bench in between classes and, of course, for his comfort a substantial and comfortable benching blanket.

Always ensure that you have several towels; these will be extremely useful if your dog should be a little travel sick or salivates profusely. Also, on a really hot day, a towel that has been thoroughly soaked in cold water and wrung out to remove excess moisture can be draped over your dog's back to prevent his becoming overheated.

Be sure to plan your journey the day before, allowing enough time to be able to complete it in comfort. There is nothing worse either for you or your dog than arriving late at the show and having to rush into the ring at the last minute.

Show bag.

In addition, I would recommend that you carry the following for any journey made during the winter months. Always be sure to have food for your dog and yourself in case you should become stranded for hours in snow. Hot drinks for yourself are essential; chocolate bars are another good idea. Take plenty of bedding both for you and your dog, together with some extra warm clothing for yourself. Strips of old carpet plus a light shovel can extricate you from many untold difficulties in heavy snow.

The Day of the Show

You are at last setting off to your first show. You know exactly where you are going, having worked out your route the day before, and have estimated approximately how long this will take you. Your charge is happily settled in the car together with all your show equipment and necessary extras, and off you go.

When you arrive at the show you will be directed, in most cases, to the exhibitors' car park where you will be able to unload. If you are travelling alone, try not to overload yourself with too many 'extras' so that the transition from car to benching tent can be accomplished in one journey. Never be tempted to leave your dog in the car on a hot day while you take all your bags and baggage to the ringside, as even a few minutes could prove fatal in a heatwave. Similarly, do not be tempted to leave your dog along on the bench while you return to get all your paraphernalia from the car, for he may become distressed and cause himself or perhaps others injury in his panic.

These first few outings to the show are going to be very strange and traumatic for him; for instance, if you leave him chained to his bench while you return to the car, he will not know that you are not abandoning him. I never leave any of my dogs unattended on their benches – if several Great Danes became agitated at the same time, their mood may be caught by others further along and untold damage could be done. Always ensure that you allow your dog to relieve himself as soon as possible in the exercise area allocated, then check to see what class you have entered him in and, most important, locate your ring well before your class.

When judging eventually begins, if you are in the first class make sure that you are ready to go into the ring. Always check that everything is prepared, that your dog has been brushed over and that he is looking the part. This is now the time and the place where your weeks of training will come to fruition.

Always be prepared and watch the judge. When you first enter the ring and each exhibit is being accounted for by the steward and any absentees noted, the judge will walk along the line having an initial look at those dogs entered under him. Have your dog standing in the correct fashion before the judge gets to you.

Some judges are inclined to throw a cursory glance around the ring in between judging each dog. By all means let your dog relax and rest, but try not to let him stand in such a position that he seems to make himself look totally deformed in any way, shape or form. This little lapse of concentration on your part may cast a seed of doubt into that judge's mind before the final assessment. This is particularly likely in the case of a novice judge or perhaps one not quite *au fait* with the breed.

If on this first occasion you do not win, try not to be downhearted, for not all the top-winning kennels that you see today have always been at the top of the tree. Everyone has to start somewhere, so carry on watching to see which types of dog that particular judge is picking out; maybe they vary in type from your own. Watch the handlers as well (especially the good ones) and learn from them. Try to see if they are doing anything that may help you in the future, or rather to help you to help your dog.

If, however, you are lucky enough to walk away with a prize card for whatever placing, then you should feel really pleased with your dog. Perhaps this may even be a red card, the ultimate and one to aspire to at this stage. If you win your class, your day is not finished for you will be required to compete against all the other unbeaten dogs at the end. Of course, if you are entered in another class, provided you remain unbeaten you will be needed to stand among the others for Best of Breed, unless it is a Championship Show when it will be a challenge for the big green card – a Challenge Certificate.

Whenever possible, that is in between classes or between winning your class and challenging at the end of the day, allow your dog to relax. When the time comes this will mean that your dog is fresh and alert, giving everything he has got to help catch the judge's eye when he is taking that all-important final look.

Ch. Vernlam Maxie of Delwin.

Unbeaten Dogs and Bitches

To compete in the final line-up you must not have been beaten by any other exhibit. There are two exceptions to this: the challenge for Best Puppy and the challenge for the Reserve Challenge Certificate.

Obviously, to compete for the Best Puppy award the dog has to be less than twelve months of age. He is entitled to compete with other puppies if he has won either a Minor or Puppy class. If, however, he has been entered in another class, for instance Junior or Maiden, and has been beaten by another dog or perhaps dogs, provided that none of the other dogs above him were puppies, he would still be entitled to compete for Best Puppy unless stated otherwise in the schedule. A good steward will realize the situation, though sometimes inexperience or perhaps a large entry with extra administrative duties for the steward may cause this to be overlooked. Therefore, always be sure to be aware of judging progress and be ready to compete when the call goes out.

Ch. Jafrak Forever Cookie. (Photo: Pearce.)

The CC will be awarded to one of the unbeaten dogs in the line-up. The Reserve CC can also be handed to one of the other dogs within this line-up or alternatively the judge may decide to call in the runner-up in the class from where the CC winner came. Therefore, if you were second in a class, especially when it is one of the major classes, for example Limit or Open, it is always advisable to be standing near the ring in case you are required.

The judge will no doubt ask you to move again and will want to take a second look at your dog, possibly handling him again. So be on your toes and be prepared!

Leaving the Show

Most shows, especially the Open and Limited ones, allow you to leave as soon as you have completed your classes. Nowadays the majority of Championship Shows also follow this routine. Some, however, give a time in the schedule which is the earliest that your dog is entitled to leave the confines of the show. In special cases dispensation can be sought from the show secretary or show manager should an emergency arise which necessitates your early departure.

When the summer is at its height and your car has been sitting for hours in the sweltering sunshine, make sure that you allow some air into it before loading up all your bags and baggage and finally your Great Dane. Have the windows wound down enough to allow plenty of ventilation into the car, but not to endanger your Dane should he have access to a window when the car is in motion. How UK exhibitors envy those in the USA who have air-conditioning as standard equipment in their cars.

When all is said and done, dog showing can provide many hours of pleasant relaxation with friends and other exhibitors while watching and discussing the breed and various aspects of it. Most people are there to compete, and we all go hoping to win. That is one of the end products of breeding and showing, producing a good or better specimen of the breed, that can hold its own amongst the cream of the country's Great Danes for everyone to see. But remember that it is not the end of the world if when the day is finished you fail to come away with a prize. Remember, above all, that the devotion and loyalty given to you by your companion is prize and reward enough; anything else is an added bonus.

6

Judging

Most people, if questioned on whether they wished to judge, would I imagine fall into three categories. The first of these would be those who would eventually like to judge our breed, if invited, after having spent a suitable period of time learning the basic 'ground rules', studying the breed both in and out of the ring.

The next group would include those who would initially decline, due to not feeling capable at that particular time of undertaking such an appointment. After a short while and a certain amount of consideration, having gained more experience, they may change their minds and decide eventually to accept an invitation.

The third and final group are fortunately only a small minority. These want to judge not only their own breed but often several others also, without first gaining the necessary experience. In days gone by, there used to be a popular saying that one should serve an apprenticeship before attempting to judge. When you think about it, this is quite sensible for it allows the aspiring judge to learn all the aspects of the breed and also the ring procedure. This can now be achieved by attending seminars and teach-ins that are arranged around the country.

In any sport or hobby that is undertaken, a certain amount of time is spent in gaining knowledge, finding out the best and most responsible way of accomplishing an end result. For instance, if you were learning to hang-glide you would not expect to partake physically without having first learnt the intricacies and various methods of adapting to this without causing yourself or perhaps others injury. The same procedure is relevant regarding judging, although of course it would not prove fatal, but without proper care and training the result could be disastrous for the breed. So spend your early years in Great Danes becoming acquainted with them and coming to learn, love and understand the breed. The more you become involved with them the more you will find there is to learn, the fascination is never-ending.

You will have to wait to be asked to judge a few classes; you cannot go around propositioning society secretaries, telling them how keen

The author with Ch. Hotpoint's Fortuna of Walkmyll (Best in Show), and Falkenburg Arcas (Reserve Best in Show), at the Scottish Great Dane Club Championship Show, 1981.

you are to judge the breed. In most cases, new judges are invited because they are seen showing their dogs, usually with reasonable success and also showing that they have a commitment to the breed.

Prior to judging your breed, you can learn about ring procedure and watch various judges at close quarters by becoming a ring steward.

Stewarding

A good ring steward can be invaluable to a judge, especially to one who has drawn a large entry. In the United Kingdom where we operate a system where dogs are able to enter in more than one class, one of the steward's main tasks is to place in correct order of merit from the results of previous classes dogs that have already been seen.

Many societies operate from their own 'bank' of regular stewards but others are often grateful for any volunteers. A word with a show manager or secretary of any particular association may eventually secure a place on their team of stewards. As a novice steward you would initially be with a steward of greater experience, who would be able to guide you through the basic duties required of a ring official.

Ch. Hotpoint's Fortuna of Walkmyll.

As a steward you will be issued on the day with a steward's board, a catalogue, rosettes and prize cards for each particular breed (if you are stewarding for more than one breed you will often be given all the necessary awards for each breed in your ring). In countries that operate under the FCI system (for example, Scandinavia and Germany) where ribbons are handed out, the steward usually has to ensure that the ribbons awarded by the judge are handed to the exhibitor.

Prior to each class it is the steward's job to call the class name/number out to the ringside. It should always be noted that it is the exhibitor's duty to ensure that they are in time for their class. It is not up to the steward to chase prospective exhibitors around the show. It is always expected that the show manager or relevant official is contacted prior to judging in order to give warning of the imminent start. This is especially important at an All Breed Show where several breeds are due to be judged in each ring.

In the UK when the dogs first enter the ring the steward's job initially is to guide them to the particular part of the ring that the judge wishes to commence from. The steward will then go along the line of exhibits with a catalogue marking those present and noting any absentees. When all the dogs gathered in the ring have been noted by the steward, the judge will then begin to assess the exhibits present. While this is under way the steward's next job is to return any unclaimed ring numbers to the steward's box. Another duty now is to ensure in the case of large classes that the exhibits are kept in formation, always checking that the next exhibit is ready for the judge to handle while the preceding dog is moving around the ring.

When all the dogs have been seen, the steward needs to be at hand ready for the judge to make his final decisions. It is advisable prior to judging to assess where the majority of onlookers are situated, confirming with the judge the position of class winners after the final decision has been reached in order that the majority of spectators are able to see the final winners.

Once the judge has completed judging the first class, the steward should have the judge's paperwork together to hand him, including the Judge's Book and notepad for any comments he will make for his critique. It is the custom for a judge in the UK to give a critique of his winners which will be eventually printed in both the main dog journals, *Dog World* and *Our Dogs*. Amongst the various bits and pieces received by the judge from the show society will be pre-addressed envelopes for both these papers.

It is standard practice that the first-place winner alone is reported on at an Open or Limited Show, whereas at a Championship Show the first two places are reported. In the case of the Open and Limited Shows record is given of the second-placed dog and his owner, while at Championship Shows this applies to third place. Therefore, when a judge has finished a class and placed the dogs in order of merit and the prizes are handed out, the appropriate winners will be asked to remain a little longer in the ring while the judge makes a few notes on them, in order to be able to expand in more detail at a later date. Everyone has their own method, sometimes it is advisable to make a note of any particular fault or point that you would have preferred the dog not to have carried. This helps to ensure that you do not go into print describing the excellence of one part of the dog's anatomy when in fact this may be something that could have been improved on.

On the Continent and in Scandinavia a judge is requested to give a critique there and then in the ring and for this purpose he is assisted by a minimum of two stewards. One of these is responsible for writing down the judge's comments on each dog as they are dictated, while

Ch. Eastlight Second Edition.

the second is devoted to ensuring that the smooth running of the ring is attended to, including the presentation of the prizes. Three copies of the judge's individual critiques are made under this system. One is given to the exhibitor at the end of judging, another goes to the society, and the final copy is retained for the Kennel Club of that particular country.

Stewards' Cards

Most societies these days provide stewards with a Steward's Card. Many experienced stewards, though, ensure that they have their own cards already drawn up. A Steward's Card is a sheet of paper with a grid of lines set out on it. Across the top, the five class placings are written while down the left-hand side are the class numbers. When the class is completed the steward records the class winners down on his card and he will be able to fill in the catalogue for the judge on completion of judging.

Having ascertained that the judge has finished with this particular class and the placings have been noted, the awards can be handed out. If there are two stewards in the ring one can be handing these out while the other is finalizing the paperwork for that class. At some of the smaller All Breed Shows there is usually only one steward to take care of everything, so one really has to be organized and methodical. In this case, the winners need to be recorded and then the prize cards can be handed out while informing the ringside in as loud a voice as possible of the relevant numbers.

When this task is completed it will then be necessary to call in the next class after having ensured that the relevant ring numbers are ready to be given out. At many of the All Breed Championship Shows in the UK, the ring numbers are left on the benches ready for the exhibitors to collect. In countries such as the USA the exhibit numbers are usually sent out to the entrants prior to the show.

In the UK, exhibitors can enter the ring in any order and stand in whichever order to be seen as they please, but in the USA they operate a more methodical system whereby the exhibits enter in number order and have to remain thus throughout the initial stages of the class judging until they are actually placed. This stops a lot of swapping and shuffling around, such as one exhibitor not wanting to be the first to walk, or another not wanting to be the last to walk.

When the new ring numbers have been handed out the steward has then a breathing space in which to bring the paperwork up to date. For instance, if only four exhibits were present when there were five places awarded, the spare prize card needs to be returned to the secretary at the end of judging.

Having completed that task the new prize cards for the class currently in session need to be sorted and placed close to hand. A good and helpful steward will also ensure that all absentees are marked in the judge's book. Time permitting, of course, another helpful task that the steward can undertake is to record the class winners in this book to save the judge time at the end of the day.

Judge's Book

The judge will be given a Judge's Book on arrival at the show, in which each class is recorded with the exhibitors' number; the new dogs are invariably entered in one colour of ink while the dogs that have been seen in previous classes are recorded in a contrasting colour. The book consists of several pages, one for each class, and these are sectioned

Ch. Dicarl the Alliance with Algwynne (taken at eighteen months).

and perforated. Each section in turn is split into five places where the class winners are recorded. These slips are eventually separated, one going on to the awards board at the ringside, the second going to the secretary's tent and a third to the Kennel Club, with the judge retaining one column in the book. At most All Breed Open and Limited Shows the judge, after completing the judging, will be handed a catalogue that has usually been marked up for him by the steward as the classes have progressed. At Breed Club Shows or All Breed Championship Shows, the judges collect their catalogues at the end of the day from the secretary of the association, and these may or may not be marked up for them.

The Judge's Book is a very important aspect for it should be the true and accurate record of the judging and placings that occurred. In the United States great care is taken with regard to this part of judging procedure for there the judge alone is responsible for his book. Each entry in this book can only be done by the judge and it is forbidden for anyone else to assist with it.

A steward is therefore a very important and integral part of dog show-ing and management, and assists towards ensuring the smooth run-ning and efficiency of the show, apart from being an asset to the judge in the ring. By extending their horizons eventually to stewarding for other breeds too, aspiring judges are able to get an idea of type and methods of handling different breeds.

Judging

An invitation to judge some classes at a All Breed Open Show is usually given by letter from the secretary of the society. (In some cases, this may be preceded by a phone call to enquire as to your availability before the official letter is sent out.) The letter will state the breed you are judging, the number of classes together with the date of the show and may also enquire as to the question of expenses.

When you start to judge your first few classes you will find that invitations will always be given in an honorary capacity. As time progresses, and depending on the society and the size and status of the show, you may be allowed to claim some expenses. It has to be said that most societies in the UK at the Open and Limit level do not offer expenses. Aspiring judges usually forgo any reimbursement in order to expand their judging expertise.

As you will already have realized by studying the Breed Standard, there is a lot to learn, so when you are thinking about the possibility of judging restrict yourself to this breed only! Remember that people spend a lot of time and money and energy when entering their dogs, preparing them for shows. Therefore, you owe it to them to commit yourself only to the breed that you have been associated with and are still learning to understand.

There are very few novice judges who will not make a mistake or, should I say, a decision that they later in the day think could have been reversed. Quite understandably, nerves play an important part in this field. If any person says that they are completely confident about carrying out their first appointment and have not experienced any trace of nerves, it could possibly be that they carry an inflated opinion of their own capabilities. There is no disgrace in being slightly appre-hensive.

Returning to your letter of invitation, you will also notice certain stipulations contained within it. Some societies demand that you do not judge the breed for a certain number of months prior to the

*The author judging in Norway. Best in Show is Int. Nord. Ch.
Hotpoint's New Treasure and Best of Sex is Int. Nord. Ch. Hotpoint's
Fortune Maker. (Photo: Moen.)*

appointment, or they may ask that you refrain from judging the breed within a certain radius. Always make sure you are clear on these points.

The Kennel Club is very insistent that any judging commitment is honoured, barring anything unforeseeable such as a grave illness, accident or serious family problems. Bad weather, of course, can play a part but only when conditions are extreme. If for any reason the judging appointment is not carried out, the person in question would then be contacted by the Kennel Club, who will have been informed by the society initially. In its capacity as ruling body, the Kennel Club may demand some proof that the circumstances warranted the non-appearance of the judge on the day of the show.

Prior to the show, the secretary will no doubt contact you by post giving you details of your entry and the time that they require you to be at the show. Most All Breed Shows run to a schedule with rings being allocated for a number of breeds, and these are taken in the order set out by the society. Some associations print this judging order in their schedule while others wait until the day of the show and give details on the showground itself. It may be that you are not first in the

Enrico vom Drawehner Wald of Asoud (German import). (Photo: Pearce.)

ring and may be following another breed, and the society will take this into account and assess the time that they feel it is necessary for you to arrive.

In the United Kingdom, there is of course nothing to stop you from arriving at the show before judging commences in all rings even if you are not due to judge until later in the day. In the United States, however, many shows are split into two sections for breeds, especially at Speciality Shows (Breed Club Shows). The first classes are known as Sweepstakes which are for puppies from six to eighteen months of age and they are followed by the regular classes. The judge who is judging the later classes is not allowed to watch the previous judge going through the Sweepstakes, in case he or she is influenced by any of the first judge's placements.

When the great day dawns and you are off to fulfil your first judging appointment always remember to have allowed yourself plenty of time to reach the show-site. Take into account that you may wish to have time to gather your thoughts when reaching the venue, refresh

Selmalda Rainbow Warrior.

yourself and have a coffee before you step into the ring. If you allow yourself this breathing space you will find it less traumatic stepping into the ring than having to rush in at the last minute to find all the exhibitors waiting for you.

Upon arriving at any show your first duty is to let the secretary know that you are on site. Within reason, keep in contact with this person until you step into the ring. They will inform you of the ring that you will be in and what they wish you to do, for example report back to them within a specified time or go straight to the ring. If you are going to be out of contact with them for any particular reason, such as having to make a phone call or going to sit in the refreshments areas, be sure to let them know where they can find you in case you are needed quickly. Always be sure to keep an eye on the ring that you have been allocated and assess the judging that is taking place there and how it is progressing. As the time draws near for you to be at hand, ensure that you are standing by so that you can step into the ring as soon as you are summoned.

Some shows are inclined not to carry a full complement of stewards and you may be asked upon your arrival as to whether or not you have brought your own steward with you. Unless your travelling companion (it is always a good idea to have company, especially at your first few appointments) is well experienced in this field I would definitely suggest that you request the society to supply you with one of their own stewards. Two novices in the ring together at the same time really isn't a good idea!

In the Ring

One of the first tasks upon entering the ring is to sign your Judge's Book; this ensures that the relevant slips that eventually go to the various departments are officially endorsed by you. When you open up the Judge's Book you will see the perforated slips in the columns. A quick signature of initial at the bottom of each will suffice.

When you are ready the steward will call in the first class – a time when 'butterflies' can be guaranteed to make an appearance! When your steward has completed the necessary checks the time has arrived for you to take a deep breath and start to judge your first class.

Walk along the line of dogs that will be standing in their show poses

Fassano Keyhole Kate.

and assess each dog individually. At this stage of the proceedings just a short time needs to be spent on each dog, taking a first overall look before you commence to handle them individually. However beautiful one looks standing, try not to make any cast-iron decisions now, but reserve your judgement until you have seen each aspect of the dog, by handling him and watching his movement.

When you have completed this first task, signal to the first exhibitor to stand his dog in front of you, away from the line of other exhibits. The puppy classes require patience and understanding on the part of the judge for some take a little while to settle down. Wait a reasonable amount of time for the exhibitor to settle the puppy into the required stance.

Once the dog is standing correctly take a long look from the side, the rear and finally approach him from the front. Be sure to let the dog see you, and try not to come up on him from behind, especially with a

Ch. Bencleves Bobcat. (Photo: Trafford.)

youngster who may become alarmed. A good approach is to hold out your hand gently, offering him the back of it to sniff and gain confidence. Most dogs have an affable temperament and will have no qualms about your handling them. If you do come across one who is decidedly unfriendly and attempts to bite, this must be immediately penalized and the dog disqualified.

Take the dog's head in your hands and take mental note of the proportions of the head properties, look at the eyes for the desired set, size and colour remembering that, although dark eyes are preferable, wall or odd eyes are allowed in harlequins. There should be very little lumpiness in the cheeks and the face should be well chiselled. The bridge of the nose should be wide with the desired slight ridge where the cartilage joins bone, which is of course a characteristic of the breed. The nostrils should be large and wide, giving the preferred blunt look to the nose, with the lips hanging squarely in the front and the ears set high on the skull and folded forward.

Having taken a look at the head, you next need to check the dog's dentition and bite either by opening the dog's mouth yourself or asking the handler to do so. The teeth should be level, with the mouth displaying a perfect scissor bite (where the upper teeth close over the lower teeth).

Run your hands down the dog's neck feeling to check that it is free from any loose skin and is well muscled and arched, eventually letting your hands run down on to and across its shoulders. The shoulders should be muscled without being overloaded and should slope well back; run your hands along them to feel the lay of the shoulderblades. Run your hands lightly down the legs, feeling for the desired strength encompassed in the bone needed to carry these powerful dogs.

When standing back you should be able to see that the body is deep with the dog's brisket reaching right down below the elbow. Run your hands over the dog's body, feeling this time the ribs which should be well sprung giving ample space within the body for the vital organs to lie comfortably, working unrestricted within good bone formation. The underside of the dog should be well drawn up under the belly with strong back and loins, and the loins should be slightly arched.

Now feel the dog's hindquarters, which should be very muscular and fit in order to give the dog the momentum he would need. The second thigh should be long with a good turn of stifle. The hocks, when viewed from behind, should be set low and should turn neither in nor out. Look at the feet of the Dane: they should be well arched with short and carefully manicured nails. This helps to ensure that the foot develops into the desired shape, with the nails preferably being dark except in harlequins where light are allowed.

The tail should be thicker at the root than towards the end and should be carried in a straight line when the dog is on the move; it should on no account curl over the dog's back. With the males of the species it is necessary to check that they are entire, that is that the dog's two testicles are fully descended into the scrotum.

Having taken a final overall look at the dog in front of you it is now time to see him go through his paces around the ring. Always, when asking the exhibits and exhibitors to move, or for that matter any other request that you may make, ensure that you are positive and clear in your definition of what you require without becoming dogmatic. A dithering and indecisive judge is no pleasure to watch in the ring and does not exude any confidence to those awaiting the final decisions.

Decide beforehand where and how you wish the dogs to move. The usual practice is to ask them to move in a triangle first of all. If you are not happy with the movement on any exhibit never be afraid to ask them to repeat the exercise in order to satisfy yourself on any point that may be troubling you.

Having gone over each exhibit and assessed their movement the time has come to place them as you see fit. Always check with your steward whether four or five places are given. If it is a very large class you may wish to pull out more than the required places in order to see them move again, or merely to assess these few that you like against each other. You should make it clear that you are not placing the dogs at this stage. Once you have reached your decision, place the dogs in the required order. Having noted down the winner's numbers while your steward attends to his duties, commence to make a few notes on the winners ready for the critique you will need to submit eventually to the dog press. The submitting of critiques to the two dog papers is not compulsory but it is expected and gives people a chance to see how you came to your decisions.

Championship Show Judging

As time goes by, you will no doubt be invited to judge the breed on other occasions. If you have higher aspirations, you may eventually be invited to judge at a Championship Show. Judging at this level gives you the right to say that in your opinion the dog and bitch to whom you have awarded the Challenge Certificates are of high enough merit to be of Champion material.

Ch. Janriche He's Daring.

In the United Kingdom, anyone who exhibits and owns dogs is entitled to judge and eventually may become a Championship Show judge. In the United States judges are licensed by the American Kennel Club and aspiring judges have to apply to the AKC for this privilege. In the United Kingdom, experience is gained for judging by undertaking a few classes in the early stages at Limited or Open Shows. As time goes on, a judge's experience should expand to include eventually a Breed Club Open Show. The Kennel Club likes its future Championship Show judges to have judged regularly and over a set period of time, that being five years at least.

When the day arrives that your invitation to judge a Championship drops through the letter box, upon perusing the letter you will see that the society ask you to accept or decline the invitation within a specified time, and you will also be required to state whether or not this is your first such appointment.

The author judging in the USA with her Best of Winners.

Replying to this as an uninitiated Championship Show judge, you will then receive a questionnaire from the society which will need to be completed, giving full details of your judging experience within the breed from the first show you ever judged. Obviously it is imperative that you always keep records of your engagements, ensuring also that you keep confirmation of these appointments in the shape of catalogues, schedules or letters from each society. Sometimes the Kennel Club asks for proof of judging experience. As the questionnaire will ask you for details of classes, entries and the number of exhibits, ensure that you have all these written down safely somewhere, too.

Having completed the form, return it as soon as possible to the society who will then forward it to the Kennel Club. Then comes a period of waiting which can last several anxious weeks. Providing that you have completed all the requirements, it is usual for the request to be successful.

Judging is an experience not to be undertaken lightly, for exhibitors are putting their trust in you to find the best dogs from within their midst.

Ch. Impton Big Sur and Impton Sierra. (Photo: Fall.)

On the other hand, you want to make it as enjoyable an experience as possible for both yourself and those who have spent their hard-earned money to enter under you.

Be pleasant and enjoy yourself (even if you are nervous initially), be fair and judge to the best of your ability. Exhibitors and spectators alike are no fools. Obviously you cannot please all the people all of the time and however good a job you feel you have done, there will always be someone who cannot resist a 'gripe'. Unfortunately, this is only human nature.

However, if you are seen to be trying to do your best the majority of people concerned will realize this. A judge who makes the odd mistake to start with always has the opportunity to learn by his mistakes in the future, whereas the judge who is seen blatantly trying to further his own career will gain few friends and, like all who try to cheat any system, will soon be found out.

7

Breeding

Successful breeding is a mixture of studying pedigrees and having an instinctive, intuitive feeling about a dog. This, of course, comes with practice and experience that can only be gained over many years of involvement with a breed.

An owner of a pet Great Dane bitch is generally discouraged by the dog's breeder from having a litter from her, unless the breeder feels that the resulting litter could be promising and that the owner is responsible enough to undertake the commitment. In these circumstances, the breeder would usually be available to offer to the owner of the bitch all their years of experience in the breed, giving guidance, help and advice along the way.

Responsibilities of Breeding

Before one even considers breeding a litter, it is important that all the implications of doing so are taken into account. Breeding can be a fascinating and rewarding hobby, but it also bears enormous responsibilities, and anyone who wishes to breed dogs must be equipped and prepared to put in the work and commitment that is necessary for the good of the litter produced – and for the good of the breed as a whole.

One of the drawbacks of breeding a litter is the cost, which includes care of the bitch before, during and after whelping, stud fees, probable veterinary fees, together with the cost of rearing the litter in the correct manner. It is extremely important that the progeny are given a good start in life, for the sake of their future well-being and condition, and for the sake of the breed, so you must be prepared to withstand the financial cost that good rearing inevitably incurs. A large dog is not always easy to home, so while you wait for suitable owners for your young puppies, you will have to continue to feed and care for them, the cost of which you may find to be prohibitively high.

Another very important aspect to consider is the sheer size of the litter, numerically that is. To produce a litter of possibly eleven puppies would be totally irresponsible if there were no possibility of good and loving homes being available for them. Prospective responsible owners need to be sought, those who have the means, commitment and environment to be able to provide one of these puppies with a good and happy home life.

Remember that not being well known within the world of Great Danes will also make a difference to your chances of finding good homes for the litter. Breeders who have been involved with the breed for many years, and have become known through breeding and showing good stock, will attract possible future owners before the unknown breeder will. An established, reputable breeder will have worked hard to build up a good reputation, so do not be under any illusion that in breeding this litter you will make your fortune; any breeder of repute will tell you that this is not the case.

No one should ever be tempted to take a bitch along to a stud-dog with the intention of letting her have one litter before she is spayed. That is certainly no good for the bitch or the resulting litter, or, equally important, for the breed.

Finally, it is extremely important that the breeding of a litter has a purpose, namely the improvement of the breed, and the breeder should be committed to producing the best possible quality in any prospective litter. No responsible breeder would produce a litter just because it seemed to be a good idea at the time.

Finding the Right Dog

If, having considered all the implications, you purchase a Great Dane with the idea that you may eventually wish to breed, the first important step is to ensure that you buy the right dog for the foundation of your kennel. So you must look for a bitch who has no outstanding fault, or faults, and – equally important – one who has good bloodlines.

There is no point in going to someone who has bred from a bitch with a pedigree that reads like a lucky dip, mated to a dog of equal repute, and buying one of the puppies from such a union just because it 'looks all right'. There is a very good saying that 'breeding will out', and out it will in future generations if the pedigree and breeding of your foundation bitch were not up to scratch. Out will come all the

Ch. Helmlake Fancy Fashion.

faults that will take a virtual lifetime to get rid of, and you will get nowhere with any breeding programme. It is worth pointing out that if, in a weak moment, you have done this, there is nothing to be gained in carrying on by taking her to one of the top stud-dogs in the country. The laws of genetics dictate that you have to have good bloodlines on both sides; the stud-dog cannot do everything, so you would be best advised to start again.

Before you reach the stage of breeding in any way, I would suggest that you do as I did initially: visit as many shows as you can, preferably Championship Shows, to see the Great Dane in all his glory. Study the show catalogue and compare the dogs that you like with their breeding stated therein. Also compare the lines of the dogs that appear to win consistently (that is, those that are placed in the first two or three of a final class line-up). A good dog should always be placed in the finalists. Compare one show with another, and gradually you will be able to identify which type keeps winning and the sort of Great Dane that you like.

Ch. Walkmyll Flare of Selmalda.

Never rush this first stage, for you should not enter into any breeding programme without being quite sure what you like, and whether it is the correct type of Dane. This is a very important decision to make because, if you are quite serious about owning and breeding Great Danes, this first choice will settle the future of your entire breeding programme. This applies equally whether you are buying a stud-dog or bitch, puppy or adult.

Discuss your choice with others who have more experience in the breed. The breeders who have the welfare of the breed at heart will generally be only too willing to give you the benefit of their knowledge and experience.

Ideally, one should breed from a bitch that can be shown and be consistently placed in the first three at a Championship Show, although it does not necessarily matter if she never wins a CC. With the careful studying of pedigrees, combined with 'gut feeling' and a certain percentage of luck, this bitch may produce the first in a line of winning dogs for you.

Another factor to be taken into consideration is, of course, finance. You are unlikely to be able to purchase the sort of bitch I describe very

Bervale Wolfgang (black). (Photo: Pearce.)

cheaply, so you must be prepared to spend as much as you can possibly afford. The investment is well worth it in order to ensure that your kennel is built on strong, good-quality foundations.

You may decide that instead of buying a bitch, you would prefer to have a male. Again, it is extremely important that you go to a reputable breeder who is prepared to sell you a good male puppy with generations of good breeding behind him. There is a fair chance that, having acquitted himself well in the ring, he will eventually prove himself at stud. But if you purchase a litter-brother from the 'lucky dip', it is extremely unlikely that you will have people queuing up to use him, even if he has won once or twice in the ring.

To produce a good show puppy, or puppies, a combination of selective, careful breeding and knowledge is required. Pedigrees, therefore, are all important: in a pedigree you should be able to see a consistent line of good breeding; you do not want to see a hotchpotch of relatively unknown lines or, for that matter, dogs.

Colour

Code of Ethics

At present, there is no UK Code of Ethics, so I shall draw your attention to the Code of Ethics drawn up by the American Great Dane Club, which simplifies the colour breeding syndrome. There are only five recognized colours, all of which fall into four colour strains:

1. Fawn and brindle.
2. Harlequin and harlequin-bred black.
3. Blue and blue-bred black.
4. Black.

Colour of Dane	Pedigree of Sire and Dam	Approved Breedings
1 Fawn	Four (4) generation pedigrees of fawn, or brindle only	1 Fawn bred to fawn
1 Brindle	Brindle Danes should not carry black, harlequin or blue upon them	1 Brindle bred to brindle or fawn only
2 Harlequin	Four (4) generation pedigrees of harlequin or harlequin-bred black Danes *should not* carry fawn, brindle or blue upon them	2 Harlequin bred to harlequin, black from harlequin breeding, or black from black breeding only
2 Black (Harlequin-bred)		2 Black from harlequin breeding bred to harlequin, black from harlequin breeding, or black from black breeding only
3 Blue	Four (4) generation pedigrees of blue or blue-bred black Danes *should not* carry fawn, brindle or harlequin upon them	3 Blue bred to blue, black from blue breeding, or black from black breeding only

3 Black (Blue-bred)		3 Black from blue breeding bred to blue, black from blue breeding, or black from black breeding only
4 Black (Black-bred)	Four (4) generation pedigrees of black-bred Danes *should not* carry fawn, brindle, harlequin or blue upon them	4 Black from black breeding bred to black, blue or harlequin only (*see* note below)

Note   Black-bred Great Danes may be bred to blacks, blues or harlequins only; puppies resulting from these breedings will be blacks or harlequins from harlequin breeding (category 2 above), blacks or blues from blue breeding (category 3 above), or blacks from black breeding (category 4 above).

It is our belief that colour mixing other than that set forth above is injurious to our breed.

All colours shall be pure colour bred for four (4) generations.

As you see, there are five recognized colours, which fall into the four colour strains.

In the fawn and brindle category, black should not be carried, nor should harlequin, nor should blue. The Code suggests that fawn should be bred to another fawn or brindle, while a brindle can be bred to another brindle or fawn.

The sire and dam of harlequin and harlequin-bred black breeding are advised not to carry any fawn, brindle or blue breeding. Harlequin should be bred only to harlequin or to a harlequin-bred black, or to a black from black breeding.

A black that is harlequin bred should be bred to another black from harlequin breeding, or to a harlequin, or to a black from black breeding. It is said that harlequins are 'a rich man's hobby'. Suffice to say that it can be challenging, fascinating, and sometimes heart-breaking to produce a truly well-marked specimen of the breed. You would think that it would be fairly easy to mate a well-marked dog to a well-marked bitch, and to achieve wonderful results, but unfortunately it is not always as simple as it sounds.

Ch. Endroma Black Magic. (Photo: Dalton.)

I have had a lifetime's experience with harlequins, having grown up with them in my native Norway. I rekindled my involvement with the Great Dane when I settled in England and started to breed here. I spent many long hours talking and listening to many knowledgeable breeders, and also travelling around to various shows. With all this extra knowledge, added to that gained in my earlier associations with Danes, I eventually started to breed harlequins for myself.

Many of the harlequins that I saw in the United Kingdom were beautifully marked, but to my mind they were not quite grand enough. They appeared to be a little too small in stature, a little too light in bone; I felt that their heads were too snipey and, for me personally, there was not enough depth of brisket. I went to Germany to see the harlequins there; this was probably the best decision I ever made, for upon this experience was set the future success of the Helmlake kennel.

On my way there, I visited the Winners Show in Amsterdam, and it was there that I saw the dog of my dreams, Int. Ch. Eick Imperial, going Best in Show. I made enquiries as to whether this beautiful dog was for sale; he was, but unfortunately the price was out of my reach. However, I bought a son of his at nine months, Ben-el-Eick von

Ch. Helmlake Chico. (Photo: Pearce.)

Forellenparadies. Although he was not as perfectly marked as I should have liked, he had everything else that I had been searching for: size, substance, movement, angulation, excellent temperament and, above all, a very strong head. I eventually mated him to Helmlake Magic Columbine of Merrowlea, who was a beautifully marked bitch of the Summerdale strain. Her grandfather was Kaster von Reidsterm, and her sire was Magic Wand of Merrowlea, an ideally marked dog. This liaison produced two perfectly marked harlequins: one became Ch. Helmlake Chico, and the other Helmlake Constant Fashion.

To say that Chico changed my life would be an understatement and, according to many experts of the time, he also changed the pattern of harlequin breeding as it was then known. This was most satisfying for me, for years of planning and patience had produced a harlequin to be really proud of. Chico sired many champions both in the UK and overseas, one notably famous progeny of his being Ch. Helmlake Fancy Fashion, who I feel was outstanding. She in turn was mated to Montego of Helmlake, who was also a Chico son and a prominent sire of harlequins, the result being Ch. Helmlake Implicable.

Ch. Helmlake Implicable.

However, with harlequin breeding, you have to be prepared to be hard, as culling part of a litter is sometimes necessary. Ninety per cent of puppies who are born pure white, or have only one or two patches, are certain to be deaf. For the sake of these puppies, and for the health and betterment of the breed, it is kinder to have them put to sleep by the vet. It is best that the decision be made as quickly as possible; postponing the decision only makes the agony worse, the older the puppy gets. If you feel that you would be unable to make this decision, it is best for you not to become involved in harlequin breeding.

In category 3 of the Code of Ethics, blues or blacks that are blue bred are discussed. It is required that they should carry four generations of blues, or blacks, that are blue bred. There should be no mix of fawn, brindle or harlequin in any of these generations. For blue, you should breed blue to blue, or blue to a black from blue breeding, or blue to a black that is black bred. For a black that is blue bred, you should breed black to blue, or black to another black of blue breeding or, alterna-

Pedigree of Ch. Helmlake Implicable

Breed Great Dane **Colour** Harlequin **Sex** Male **Date of Birth** 29 August 1978

Parents	Grandparents	Great Grandparents	G–G Grandparents
Sire Montego of Helmlake (harle)	**Sire** Ch. Helmlake Chico (harle)	**Sire** Helmlake Ben el Eick v. Forellenparadies (harle)	**Sire** Int. Ch. and B.S. 69 Ch. Luxemburg 69 Eick Imperial **Dam** Mara v. Furst Bismarck
		Dam Helmlake Magic Columbine of Merrowlea (harle)	**Sire** Magic Wand of Merrowlea **Dam** Summerdale Elaine
	Dam Leslie's Taura v. Glenbrae (black imp. U.S.A.)	**Sire** Count Igor v. Meistersinger (harle)	**Sire** Am. Ch. The Dutchman v. Meistersinger **Dam** Schatzi v. Meistersinger
		Dam Ch. Leslie's Raggedy Anne (harle)	**Sire** Orellis Brede v. Waldesruh **Dam** Am. Ch. Mountdania's Nifty Number
Dam Ch. Helmlake Fancy Fashion (harle)	**Sire** Ch. Helmlake Chico (harle)	**Sire** Helmlake Ben el Eijck v. Forellenparadies (harle)	**Sire** Int. Ch. and B.S. 69 Ch. Luxemburg 69 Eick Imperial **Dam** Mara v. Furst Bisamarck
		Dam Helmlake Magic Columbine of Merrowlea (harle)	**Sire** Magic Wand of Merrowlea **Dam** Summerdale Elaine
	Dam Bettina of Helmlake (harle)	**Sire** Helmlake Ben el Eick v. Forellenparadies (harle)	**Sire** Int. Ch. and B.S. 69 Ch. Luxemburg 69 Eick Imperial **Dam** Mara v. Furst Bismark
		Dam Helmlake Ulanova el Eick v. Furst Bismarck (harle)	**Sire** Int. Ch. Eick Imperial **Dam** Inca v. Furst Bismarck

tively, black to a black from black breeding. Finally, a black that is black bred should, as with the other categories, carry the required four generations of designated breeding; this time it states that it should be black breeding (black is black). These lines should not carry any hint of fawn, brindle, harlequin or blue. However, you may breed black to black, which is fairly straightforward, or you may breed to a blue or to a harlequin. The combination of the black and harlequin breeding will result in blacks or blues, while black to black will, or should, produce black.

Line-Breeding

Line-breeding is the system of breeding adopted by most breeders for most matings. It involves breeding dogs that are related to each other, but not too closely. There are several good combinations that can be

Helmlake Quartz Fashion.

used. For instance, grandfather to granddaughter, half-brother to half-sister, uncle to niece. This should not be confused with inbreeding (*see* below). With line-breeding, you are attempting to make the most of good established lines while keeping a safe distance, so to speak.

As you will see from Ch. Helmlake Implicable's pedigree, he is the result of a half-brother to half-sister mating. Ch. Helmlake Chico is the father of both Montego of Helmlake and Helmlake Fancy Fashion. Consequently, Ben-el-Eick von Forellenparadies appears in the pedigree also. However, if you look further back in the pedigree, you will see that he is also the sire of Fancy Fashion's dam Bettina of Helmlake while her dam, Helmlake Ulanova el Eick von Furst Bismarck, is a daughter of Int. Ch. Eick Imperial. This pedigree shows what is meant by line-breeding. As time goes on and you become more and more immersed in the dog world, you will come to know the importance of breeding programmes and the significance of pedigrees, and realize why they need such careful attention.

Inbreeding

Inbreeding means mating together closely related dogs, for instance sister to brother, mother to son, father to daughter. By breeding in this way, you are constantly doubling up on your lines. The object of this method is to double up on the good points, which of course it does, but unfortunately, it also doubles up on the bad points. Nature cannot prevent faults coming out, and whilst the resulting litter is likely to have many virtues, it is also likely to have many faults – more than could be expected from a litter produced by line-breeding. In conclusion, inbreeding is not a course to be recommended.

Outcrossing

I believe profoundly in outcrossing, which can best be defined as introducing 'hybrid vigour'. By referring to the pedigree of Ch. Helmlake Implicable, you will see that his grandmother, Leslie's Taura v. Glenbrae, is an outcross: her line does not appear anywhere else in the pedigree, so she has effectively introduced new blood – new vigour – into the breeding. I believe that if you do not bring in new blood occasionally, you will lose size and bone. However, it is important not to use outcrosses too often, because if there are too many lines in a pedigree, it makes it extremely difficult to determine the likely characteristics of the progeny that result from an intended mating.

Experienced breeders know when to use an outcross, and what effect it will have, but the novice is best advised to avoid outcrossing until he has gained a deep knowledge of the bloodlines that he is already using.

Breeding a Litter

Let us assume that you have bought a bitch, maybe as a puppy, from a respected breeder and perhaps you have even shown her a little. It could well be that the breeder of your bitch feels that she could produce a very promising litter if put to a certain stud-dog of the breeder's choice. The breeder may even want to keep one of the offspring for himself in order to extend the line another generation.

I advise that a Great Dane bitch is not mated before she is approximately two years of age. At this age, she will have been given the chance to grow into the animal that she was bred to be, having enjoyed

Mrs Harms Cooke and her team of Champions. (Photo: Pearce.)

all the fun and freedom of her puppyhood and adolescence. She will have reached the time when she is mature enough, physically and mentally, to settle down to the task of motherhood.

When the time comes to mate her, you must ensure that she is in top condition. She must not be overweight, or underweight, and she should be checked to ensure that she has no internal or external parasites. It is wise to worm a bitch before mating as a matter of course, and to have your veterinary surgeon check her general health and condition.

The Bitch's Season

On average, a bitch will come into season once every six months, and this will usually start at the age of about nine months. The initial sign of the commencement of a season is a show of blood from the vulva. This show is commonly known as 'colour'. To begin with, it will be quite light in colour and volume, but as the season progresses, it will become more obvious. Colour will last for approximately eleven days, and towards the end of this time, it will become less apparent, eventually disappearing altogether. From the first day of colour, the vulva will begin to swell a little until, by the tenth or eleventh day, it will have increased quite dramatically in size.

When the bitch first comes into season, place your finger on the outer edge of the vulva at the top and you will feel that it is fairly firm. When the same operation is carried out around the eleventh day, you will feel a distinct softening. This, together with the disappearance of the blood, is a sure sign that the female is near her time to be mated. If you also touch her near the base of her tail, at the top of the thigh, she will 'swish' her tail to the side; this is known in the canine fraternity as 'tailing', and is another pointer that the time for her to meet her mate is drawing near.

Choosing a Stud-dog

It has to be said that breeding is a gamble, whichever way you look at it. Dogs are not machines or computers into which you can feed all the information that you have at your disposal in order to produce the desired result. However, careful planning, studying and comparing lines, including the achievements of the various progeny of the prospective sire, can cut down the odds quite considerably.

This is why it is so important that you acquire your Great Dane from someone who is caring, knowledgeable and responsible, for such a breeder will always be prepared to guide and advise you. When the time comes for you to choose a sire, you must be careful in your selection and heed the advice of your bitch's breeder, who will be of invaluable assistance in helping you to make a choice that will bring out the best in your bitch. This is something that can be learnt only through years of experience in being associated with the breed.

Having identified the stud-dog that you would most like to use for your bitch, you must first approach his owner and enquire as to whether you may bring your bitch to him. Ask a few questions, for instance, is the dog at public stud? He may be at limited stud, restricted to use on only very carefully selected bitches. Another important question is the stud fee. These factors are very important and should be dealt with well before your bitch is due to be mated. I would also suggest that you ask for a copy of the stud-dog's pedigree. Many helpful Dane owners or breeders will probably ask to see the pedigree of your bitch, and will advise you on whether or not the two lines will complement each other. They may own more than one stud-dog, and may feel that one of their other males will suit your bitch better, so do not be afraid to consult them on this, for anyone who has the betterment of the breed at heart will be happy to help and advise you.

When the time comes and your bitch is showing the very first signs of colour, contact the owner of the prospective sire as quickly as possible to ask if the dog is free to be used on your bitch. If for some reason he is unavailable, having for instance been booked to another bitch, the owner may suggest another dog that may be equally suitable.

As the time draws on, keep a close eye on your bitch incase she suddenly shows signs of losing colour. This is not an unusual occurrence, but it could mean that she needs to be mated sooner rather than later. Always keep the prospective sire's owner informed of any sudden change of pattern, and try, if at all possible, to give twenty-four hours' notice before you arrive on the doorstep with your bitch.

The Mating

On the day of the mating, try to organize yourself so that you can arrive punctually at the stud-dog's home without having had to race around causing both you and your bitch unnecessary stress. On arrival, allow your bitch to stretch her legs and encourage her to relieve herself.

Introduce the dog and bitch to each other and allow them to greet

Ch. Simba of Helmlake. (Photo: Pearce.)

each other. Do not hurry this process. However, this introduction should be conducted under strict control, with both dog and bitch on a lead, so that if either of them becomes too boisterous, or even aggressive, the handlers can separate them.

Being a massive breed as far as size and construction are concerned, the act of mating may need the assistance of a few people in order to achieve a successful result. The stud-dog is likely to be extremely heavy so, when he is on top of the bitch, at least two other people will be required to help.

One person is required to stand at the front end of the bitch, and hold her head to restrain her from turning on the dog if she becomes worried or stressed. Another person is needed to hold the dog and manually guide him if necessary, while a third assistant would help to take some of the weight off the bitch when the two are at the point of becoming 'tied'. The tie is the term used to describe the point when the stud-dog has successfully penetrated the bitch and has begun to swell

Ch. Dicarl Who's Free.

inside the vagina. The bitch's vaginal muscles then grasp the penis causing the male to ejaculate his sperm.

Once the dogs have tied, the dog will usually try to turn himself round in order to assume a tail-to-tail position with the bitch. This is a far more comfortable position for them, particularly if the tie turns out to be a long one, and is quite normal. Carefully help the dog to turn, making sure that the bitch's tail is not in the way as he does this.

The dog will not be able to withdraw until the bitch's muscles relax and allow him to do so. You cannot induce the tie to break, and it is important that the two dogs do not try to separate before the tie ceases naturally, as this will cause the dog pain and possibly injure one or both animals. So, especially with a maiden bitch (one who has not been mated before), who may try to pull away too early, ensure that the dogs stay together until the tie is over.

The tie can last for anything from a few minutes to a back-breaking length of time (usually for you, rather than the dog). If the tie is short in duration, or even appears not to have occurred, it does not necessarily mean that the bitch will not conceive. The two most important factors in effecting conception are that the stud-dog is potent and that the bitch is brought to him on the right day when she is ready to conceive.

Most stud-dog owners offer a second service, and in most cases this occurs two days after the first one. However, it is unwise to assume that the second service will be offered automatically, so this should be discussed at the time of booking. Very often, a maiden bitch will be more receptive to the second mating, because she will have settled down and be less nervous about the proceedings.

With a maiden bitch, there is also the question of her having to be 'broken down'. This happens when the stud-dog enters her and breaks the hymen, which can cause her to cry out and is quite natural. However, if preferred, this can be done before the mating by a breeder who is highly experience in such matters. In order to do this, hands and fingernails must be scrupulously clean. For reasons of hygiene and the bitch's comfort, it is necessary to lubricate two fingers with an antiseptic oil or lubricant. The fingers are then inserted into the bitch's vagina in order to produce the result that the dog would have done on entering. Of course, this operation should be carried out by someone experienced, and should never be attempted by anyone with little knowledge of breeding.

There are various trains of thought regarding this method. Some say that it is unhygienic and can sometimes result in an infection being passed to the bitch through unclean nails. Others, however, advocate this method in the opinion that, if done at a quiet time before the bitch meets the dog, it is less stressful for the bitch at the moment of inter-course.

If you have a maiden bitch, it is advisable to take her to an experi-enced stud-dog, who will not cause the bitch unnecessary and additional stress by becoming over-excited and clumsy. Similarly, an untried stud-dog should be taken to a matron bitch, who will not hin-der the inexperienced dog's first efforts.

The stud fee is payable immediately after the mating has taken place. A Litter Registration Form should be completed and signed by the owner of the stud-dog, and given to the owner of the bitch. Without this, the litter cannot be registered.

Misalliance

A misalliance is an unplanned mating. It usually takes place when a bitch has what is termed a 'silent season', when she is capable of mating and conceiving, but shows no sign of being in season – no swelling and no blood. She may then mate naturally with any dog who can gain temporary access to her. This might be a litter-brother, or may even be a dog of another breed who may be in the vicinity. If you are lucky enough to witness the mating, you will be able to prevent a pregnancy by taking the bitch to the vet who will give her a hormone injection to prevent implanation of the fertilized eggs in the uterus. However, this injection is only effective if it is given within three days of the mating. It will also bring the bitch's season on again, so obviously the bitch must be kept away from any dogs during this time.

8

Pregnancy and Whelping

Pregnancy

From the day of mating to the day of whelping is sixty-three days. This is not a hard-and-fast rule, for some bitches may not go the full duration while others may go over their time. When you initially mate your bitch, it is always advisable to inform your veterinary surgeon and, most importantly, to tell him the expected date of whelping. If your vet has been given prior warning, he will be prepared should you need any advice or consultation during the delivery. While most whelpings take place without any problems, complications can occur which require the help of a vet.

Once your bitch has been successfully mated, you will need to keep a close eye on her over the following few weeks. Everyone has a favourite method of deciding whether or not the bitch is in whelp. Some people feel that a sticky discharge appearing within a week of mating is a clear sign that all is going well. One of the surest signs is the appearance of a clearish but thick and sticky discharge around the fourth to fifth week after mating. Since Great Danes are quite particular about keeping themselves clean, this sign can easily be missed. However, if there is any sign of a dark, smelly discharge, you should immediately consult your veterinary surgeon, for something may have gone wrong and will need attention as soon as possible.

Another clear indication that a bitch is pregnant is the enlargement and increased prominence of her teats, in preparation for feeding her young. Very often, at around this time, the bitch will go off her food, and it may be necessary to tempt her with various healthy delicacies in order to persuade her to eat at all. In most cases, her appetite will return within a few days, and then may even swing to the opposite extreme whereby she becomes difficult to satisfy.

If you discover that your bitch has failed to become pregnant, you will find that most caring and respected breeders will offer a free return service to the dog.

Jan → Mar

Jan	Mar
1	5
2	6
3	7
4	8
5	9
6	10
7	11
8	12
9	13
10	14
11	15
12	16
13	17
14	18
15	19
16	20
17	21
18	22
19	23
20	24
21	25
22	26
23	27
24	28
25	29
26	30
27	31
28	Apr 1
29	2
30	3
31	4

Feb → Apr

Feb	Apr
1	5
2	6
3	7
4	8
5	9
6	10
7	11
8	12
9	13
10	14
11	15
12	16
13	17
14	18
15	19
16	20
17	21
18	22
19	23
20	24
21	25
22	26
23	27
24	28
25	29
26	30
27	May 1
28	2

Mar → May

Mar	May
1	3
2	4
3	5
4	6
5	7
6	8
7	9
8	10
9	11
10	12
11	13
12	14
13	15
14	16
15	17
16	18
17	19
18	20
19	21
20	22
21	23
22	24
23	25
24	26
25	27
26	28
27	29
28	30
29	31
30	June 1
31	2

Apr → June

Apr	June
1	3
2	4
3	5
4	6
5	7
6	8
7	9
8	10
9	11
10	12
11	13
12	14
13	15
14	16
15	17
16	18
17	19
18	20
19	21
20	22
21	23
22	24
23	25
24	26
25	27
26	28
27	29
28	30
29	July 1
30	2

May → July

May	July
1	3
2	4
3	5
4	6
5	7
6	8
7	9
8	10
9	11
10	12
11	13
12	14
13	15
14	16
15	17
16	18
17	19
18	20
19	21
20	22
21	23
22	24
23	25
24	26
25	27
26	28
27	29
28	30
29	31
30	Aug 1
31	2

June → Aug

June	Aug
1	3
2	4
3	5
4	6
5	7
6	8
7	9
8	10
9	11
10	12
11	13
12	14
13	15
14	16
15	17
16	18
17	19
18	20
19	21
20	22
21	23
22	24
23	25
24	26
25	27
26	28
27	29
28	30
29	31
30	Sept 1

July → Sept

July	Sept
1	2
2	3
3	4
4	5
5	6
6	7
7	8
8	9
9	10
10	11
11	12
12	13
13	14
14	15
15	16
16	17
17	18
18	19
19	20
20	21
21	22
22	23
23	24
24	25
25	26
26	27
27	28
28	29
29	30
30	Oct 1
31	2

Aug → Oct

Aug	Oct
1	3
2	4
3	5
4	6
5	7
6	8
7	9
8	10
9	11
10	12
11	13
12	14
13	15
14	16
15	17
16	18
17	19
18	20
19	21
20	22
21	23
22	24
23	25
24	26
25	27
26	28
27	29
28	30
29	31
30	Nov 1
31	2

Sept → Nov

Sept	Nov
1	3
2	4
3	5
4	6
5	7
6	8
7	9
8	10
9	11
10	12
11	13
12	14
13	15
14	16
15	17
16	18
17	19
18	20
19	21
20	22
21	23
22	24
23	25
24	26
25	27
26	28
27	29
28	30
29	Dec 1
30	2

Oct → Dec

Oct	Dec
1	3
2	4
3	5
4	6
5	7
6	8
7	9
8	10
9	11
10	12
11	13
12	14
13	15
14	16
15	17
16	18
17	19
18	20
19	21
20	22
21	23
22	24
23	25
24	26
25	27
26	28
27	29
28	30
29	31
30	Jan 1
31	2

Nov → Jan

Nov	Jan
1	3
2	4
3	5
4	6
5	7
6	8
7	9
8	10
9	11
10	12
11	13
12	14
13	15
14	16
15	17
16	18
17	19
18	20
19	21
20	22
21	23
22	24
23	25
24	26
25	27
26	28
27	29
28	30
29	31
30	Feb 1

Dec → Feb

Dec	Feb
1	2
2	3
3	4
4	5
5	6
6	7
7	8
8	9
9	10
10	11
11	12
12	13
13	14
14	15
15	16
16	17
17	18
18	19
19	20
20	21
21	22
22	23
23	24
24	25
25	26
26	27
27	28
28	Mar 1
29	2
30	3
31	4

Gestation table. First column lists mating date; second column lists whelping date.

Ch. Walkmyll Duncan. (Photo: Pearce.)

Care of the Brood-Bitch

From the time that you know she is in whelp, you will need to ensure that your bitch has all the extra nourishment that is necessary to help the litter growing within her. Her meals will eventually have to be split so that she is fed little and often. A recognized multivitamin additive recommended by your vet or breeder can be added to the dog's meals daily. She will also need a calcium supplement which can be given in the form of milk and bonemeal; or in the form of a proprietary brand of liquid supplement. The latter is very easy to give, either by pouring it over her food or by giving it directly into the mouth by the way of a needleless syringe. It is always advisable to step up the dosage to approximately double quantities a couple of days prior to the whelping, as this will lessen the chance of eclampsia occurring (*see* page 173). However, as with any supplements, it is extremely important not to disregard the manufacturer's dosage instructions, without first con-

161

sulting your vet, as too much can be as detrimental to the bitch as too little.

Many breeders lay great store in various homeopathic remedies to aid easy whelping, such as raspberry-leaf tablets, which have produced very good results. They can be purchased from any homeopathic shop or from shows at some of the canine trade stands that specialize in this sort of treatment.

It is always a good idea to carry on with her daily routine exercise, although she may slow down a bit as she becomes heavier. Continuing to take her on her regular walks will help to maintain a degree of fitness so that when the time comes for her to settle down and produce the litter, she should be in the peak of condition.

Preparation

Whelping Box

When the day of whelping is drawing near, it is always a good idea to introduce her to the place where you wish her to have the puppies. Some breeders prefer their bitches to have their litters in well-insulated whelping rooms or kennels set aside for the purpose, where all the necessary equipment can be kept to hand. Personally, I like the bitch to have her litter in the house. In fact, the newborn litter's first awareness of the big wide world when they first focus their sight is my bedroom. I place a large whelping box in view of my bed so that, should I be resting when labour starts, I can be there immediately.

The whelping box is a four-sided bed with a slightly raised guard rail which lines the inside of the box. This is just high enough to prevent the bitch from inadvertently rolling on the puppies, an easy way for a litter to be accidently and prematurely killed. The box can be slightly raised off the floor to stop any chill that can quickly cause hypothermia.

Another important part of the whelping equipment is the infra-red lamp, which is suspended just above the place where the litter is in repose. In this position, the lamp allows the mother to get away from its warmth while the litter can still feel the benefit of it. This is especially important when a bitch whelps in outside accommodation; hypothermia is one of the biggest causes of puppy mortality, but with care, attention and common sense, it can easily be avoided.

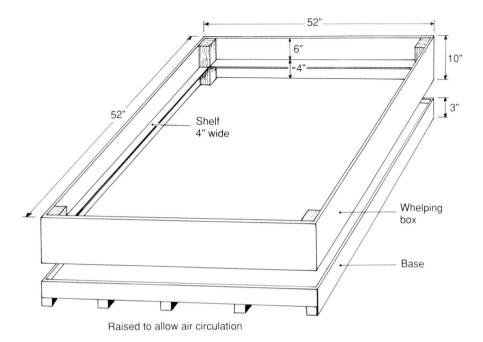

Whelping box.

Temperature Check

Approximately one week before the time your bitch is due to have her puppies, take her temperature. This is accomplished by inserting a thermometer into the rectum. If you are at all unsure of this procedure, I would suggest that you consult either your veterinary surgeon or the bitch's breeder, who will have experience in such matters. It is advisable to have a thermometer put aside purely for use on dogs. There are some extremely 'user-friendly', well-made, digital thermometers on the market which can be obtained from any major chemist; they are more substantial than the normal household ones that we have become used to over the years.

The reason for taking the bitch's temperature is to ascertain her average body heat, so that you can compare it with her temperature when labour is about to start. The average body temperature of any dog is 101.5 °F (38.6 °C). When labour is imminent, the bitch's temperature will slowly start to drop. It usually bottoms out at approximately

99 °F (37 °C). This is only a rough guide since the exact temperature will depend on the individual bitch for they all differ slightly.

Equipment

The next step is to ensure that everything is set out ready for the moment when the bitch starts to produce the first puppy. You will need the following equipment within easy reach of the whelping box:

Scissors	Bowl (for antiseptic solution)
Cotton wool	Reel of cotton (for tying umbilical cord)
Surgical clamp	Towels
Large cardboard box	Heating pad or covered hot-water bottle
Antiseptic lubricant	Vetbed, blankets and newspapers

A few days before the birth is due to take place, ensure that the whelping-box floor has been lined with newspapers. Your bitch may have taken to sleeping in the box anyway, so the newspapers should already have been laid beneath the blankets. Check also that you have a stack of extra newspapers close at hand for, as each puppy is born, a great deal of fluid is passed with both it and the placenta, so for obvious reasons fresh papers need to be readily available.

The cardboard box is used for putting whelps in while the mother gets on with producing the rest of the litter. Once labour has started, place the freshly filled hot-water bottle or heating pad in the box, and cover it with Vetbed or a similar type of simulated sheepskin blanketing. This type of bedding is especially suitable for this purpose as it remains dry and warm after puppies have urinated on it (the fibres allow fluid to filter through to the newspaper underneath, leaving the blanket dry on top).

Whelping

As the time draws near, it is important to keep an eye on the behaviour of the bitch. This is a time when your social calendar needs to be kept free of any engagements. Having informed your veterinary surgery of the due date, the practice will be on semi-standby should you need to call them. Always be sure to record the first day that the puppies are due. If nothing appears to be happening on that day, ring your vet to make an appointment to see him so that he can check that all is well.

Usually one of the first signs that labour is starting is loss of appetite accompanied by increasing restlessness. Having said this, it is not unknown for a mother-to-be to eat a healthy supper and then a few hours later produce her litter. But if she follows the normal pattern, her appetite will decrease about twenty-four hours prior to whelping. Shortly after this, she will start to become restless, and not want to be left for a minute. She will also start to pant quite dramatically and, as the whelping draws nearer, excessively, at the same time looking wild-eyed and unsettled.

One of the simplest ways to assess how the first stages of labour are progressing is to take her temperature. As she begins to follow the whelping pattern, her temperature will drop from her average (which you will have ascertained a week earlier), to about 99 °F (37 °C). You will need to take her temperature at fairly regular intervals to see how she is progressing. When the temperature has bottomed out, it will begin to rise again slowly. It is at about this time that things should start to happen, so the bitch should not be left for a moment as she may have her litter at any time now.

Daneways Cherokee Chief. (Photo: Pearce.)

The signs I have described so far are those of first-stage labour. In order to produce the puppies, the bitch needs to move the puppies down into the birth canal towards the entrance of the vagina. She does this by means of contractions, and this is the second stage.

Contractions are easily visible to the human eye and can most simply be described as strong ripples running along the bitch's back and sides towards her hindquarters as she strains to bring out her puppies. I think that at this point, most breeders feel helpless and are mere onlookers. All being well with no complications, and with the attentions of you as midwife, she should soon be the mother of several hungry mouths.

As the second stage continues, she may want to relieve herself outside. Go with her and be very vigilant, watching her every move. If it is dark, be sure to take a torch with you, for it has been known for a puppy to be born in the garden unnoticed; as the bitch squats to urinate, she may discharge a puppy at the same time. When she wants to go outside, it is always advisable to go armed with a towel in case this happens.

Prior to the first puppy's arrival into the world will come the waterbag, though in some cases the waterbag and puppy can come together. It can best be described as a large dark or greyish bubble appearing from the vulva. When it is seen, it should be allowed to disperse naturally as the bitch passes it; you should never be tempted to burst it for the first puppy may be directly behind it. When the waterbag appears, be ready with towels to deal with the first whelp. All being well, the puppy will be passed by the dam and will be completely immersed in its membranous sac with the placenta attached. Some bitches try to break open the sac surrounding the youngster. Try to dissuade them and do it yourself, because if the bitch is too slow, the puppy may drown in the fluid, and if she is too rough, she may hurt or even kill the pup. Make sure that the puppy is released as soon as possible from its bag and that nothing is covering its airways.

You must make sure that the puppy is healthy and breathing properly. Rub the puppy vigorously along its body and chest with the clean towel until you hear its first cry of life. Some puppies cry almost as soon as they come into the environment, but you should be prepared for the ones that do not; they need a lot of work and care to start them on their way.

You must ensure that the puppy's airways are clear of any fluid. If left, fluid can seep into the lungs and soon cause complications which could be fatal. In order to be sure that there is no fluid within, hold the puppy firmly in both hands, making sure that the placenta or after-birth is safely held close to the puppy. Stand with your legs slightly apart. Hold the puppy high in your hands, above shoulder level, and then swing it down between your knees. After this movement, look at the puppy to see if any excess fluid has come from the mouth and nose. If so, wipe it clean and then repeat the procedure until it appears to be clear.

The next thing to be done is to sever the cord. It is preferable that you should do this; try not to let the bitch do it herself because she may sever it too near the pup's stomach, causing tearing and injury, and hernias may be caused if she pulls too hard on it.

Take a point in the cord approximately one and a half inches ($3\frac{1}{2}$ cm) from the puppy's body and squeeze it, pushing any fluid towards the body. Take your reel of cotton thread and tie a length round the cord here, securing the thread with a knot; then cut the thread. The cord can now be severed at this point with sterile scissors, obviously on the side away from the puppy.

Once this has been accomplished, let the bitch have her first puppy so that it may take its first fill of mother's milk, which contains the colostrum necessary for its future well-being. Allowing the puppy to suckle now will also give the bitch time to become accustomed gradually to what could be many more puppies to come.

Sometimes, you have only just enough time to do this before the next puppy makes its entrance. Because of this, especially if you are inexperienced, I would suggest that you have another person with you at this time. Do not, however, have lots of people around you, for your bitch needs to be able to concentrate on what she is doing and may be disconcerted or stressed by an audience, especially of strangers. It is a well-known fact that a bitch can stop the whelping process if she is unhappy with aspects of her surroundings.

In between puppies, offer the mother a drink of milk or water, whichever she prefers, laced with a little glucose to help keep her energy level up. Also, between each puppy, she may wish to go into the garden to stretch her legs and relieve herself. Always go with her to check that she does not suddenly present a puppy in the middle of the lawn.

When it seems obvious that the second puppy is about to be born, try to remove the first puppy to the safety and warmth of the card-board box, which should have been warmed up with the hot-water

Int. Ch. Hotpoint's Be My Joy. (Photo: S. Moen.)

bottle prior to the first puppy's arrival. All being well, the bitch will not worry too much about this puppy's disappearance as she will be too involved in producing the next. However, if she does become agitated when you attempt to do this then leave well alone; just keep an eye on the firstborn to ensure that it comes to no harm while its mother gives birth to its littermate. It is all too easy for a stressed bitch inadvertently to crush one of her whelps if adequate care is not taken.

It is difficult to tell when a bitch has finished whelping, but if she is happy and relaxed for two hours without producing further puppies, it is time to call the vet who will examine her to ensure that all is well. He may give an injection of oxytocin to induce her to expel any remaining puppies or residue. Always ask the vet to come to you.

Whelping Complications

Breech Birth

With the normal presentation of a puppy, the whelp will work its way down from one of the two uterine horns, then it will pass through the uterus and from there towards the entrance of the vagina. Puppies will normally proceed head first, but in some cases they present themselves rear end first. This is known as a breech birth.

Breech presentation can cause problems, especially to one who is not fully *au fait* with general whelping procedures, as the bitch will have difficulty in producing the puppy. She will inevitably require help from you in order to deliver it as quickly and safely as possible.

As soon as enough of the puppy is visible to you, with the aid of a clean towel take hold of the body and, as each contraction comes, pull the puppy in a downward direction. You need to pull the puppy in the direction of the bitch's back legs in order to follow the formation of the birth canal, and this is easier to understand if you imagine that the bitch is standing. *Never* attempt to pull the puppy unless the bitch is contracting at the same time. It is extremely dangerous. If you cannot deliver the puppy fairly quickly, contact your vet urgently.

Releasing a Leg

Sometimes a puppy can become lodged as a result of one of its legs becoming stuck. When this happens, you will usually find that the head or posterior is produced, but nothing further happens despite some healthy straining by its mother. Immediate assistance is required to prevent the bitch from becoming overstressed or exhausted.

Lubricate one clean finger with some antiseptic solution. Slip your finger under the puppy and inside the bitch to try to ascertain the cause of the problem. This may necessitate slightly pushing the puppy back into the bitch (if the membrane has broken around the puppy's head, great care must be taken for the puppy could easily drown in the fluid produced). Try to locate the lodged limb and ease it free with your finger so that it no longer restricts the safe passage of the puppy. If you cannot ascertain the problem immediately, call your vet. When the puppy is eventually produced, treat it in the same way as the first-born, which may now be returned to its mother (keeping a watchful eye on it) while you quickly take of the newly born pup.

Uterine Inertia

There are two types of uterine inertia: primary and secondary.

Primary Uterine Inertia

With this condition, the bitch will start to display all the signs of first-stage labour: loss of appetite, panting, restlessness, and a troubled expression; her temperature will have dropped and may slowly start to rise again. Just when you think that all is going to plan, nothing further happens. The bitch very often appears to return to normal and shows no signs of wishing to produce a litter. Immediate veterinary attention is needed if the litter is to be saved, for she will go no further with the whelping once she has reached this stage. In some cases, an injection of hormone may stimulate contractions, but in others Caesarean section will be necessary.

Secondary Uterine Inertia
This condition occurs in second-stage labour. The bitch will repeatedly strain throughout a long labour, and yet produce no puppies (or no further puppies if inertia starts half-way through the whelping). Sometimes a waterbag may be produced, but nothing else. Eventually the contractions become weaker as the bitch becomes exhausted. It is usually caused by an obstruction, a puppy may have become lodged or is being presented in an awkward fashion; or if it has been a long whelping, with perhaps a large litter, sheer exhaustion may get the better of the bitch. In all cases, veterinary intervention – usually a Caesarean – is necessary to produce the litter.

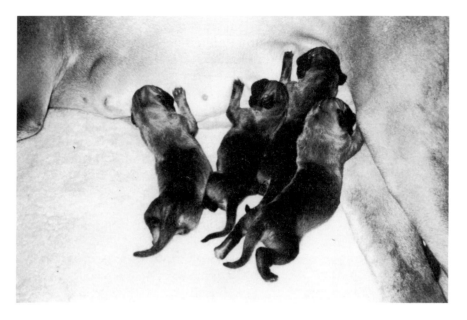

A happily feeding litter.

Ch. Metrella Academus. (Photo: Gascoigne.)

On average, the delivery of a puppy can take anything from thirty minutes to a couple of hours, although it is not unheard of for delivery to take longer than this. If a bitch has been straining incessantly for two hours with no sign of a puppy being produced, contact your vet immediately for his advice.

Caesarean Section

Fortunately, Caesarean sections are seldom required with this breed; in the vast majority of cases, Great Dane bitches have uncomplicated, natural whelpings. But occasionally, for some reason that cannot always be foreseen, the operation becomes necessary. The operation has to be carried out at the veterinary surgery. If the bitch has already produced one or more puppies naturally, you will need to ensure that they are placed in their warm box in a safe place for the duration of their dam's operation. Keep them away from the curiosity of young children, animals, and obviously out of any chill or draughts.

Make sure that you have plenty of sheets and blankets in the car for the homeward journey for, assuming that your vet decides to perform a Caesarean, the dam will need to be kept warm to prevent her from going into shock. You will also need a separate box containing blankets and a hot-water bottle for the puppies that will be returning with you.

When the bitch returns home after the operation, she will want to sleep off the effects of the anaesthetic. Place her blankets in the whelping box, and settle her down so that she is warm and cosy. Place a light blanket over her to keep her temperature from dropping and, as she becomes more aware, slowly introduce the puppies to her allowing them to suckle.

She will no doubt be confused and drowsy and may be wary of the litter, especially if none of them was produced naturally. Never leave her alone with them until you are utterly sure that she is quite happy and loving with them. It is better to be safe than sorry, even if you are exhausted and have not slept for twenty-four hours. When a bitch has produced some of the litter naturally, prior to the Caesarean, the introduction of the rest of the litter does not usually present too much of a problem.

Introducing the Puppies to the Dam
Taking each puppy individually, introduce it to one of the mother's teats, ensuring that it is well 'locked on' before progressing to the next of the litter. Signs that a puppy is feeding contentedly are that its tail will turn downwards and its front paws will press into the dam's side as it feeds.

Especially during the first few days, make sure that each puppy is having its fair share of milk and that the less boisterous ones are not being left behind. In the case of a large litter, you may need to supplement their feed for the dam is often hard pressed to provide enough food for her hungry brood (see page 174).

Never leave the mother while she is still groggy; she may want to relieve herself, or she may in her stupor accidentally squash one of her puppies. When she is quite relaxed and recovered from the trauma, you too can relax a little.

Usually, the veterinary surgeon who did the operation will want to see her within twenty-four hours to make sure that everything is going well. He will arrange to come to the house; unless anything drastic happens, you should never take her to the surgery while she is feeding a litter. After a short period of time, usually ten days, the vet will arrange for the stitches to be removed.

Postnatal Problems

Post-Whelping Metritis

A green discharge, which quickly darkens in colour to a reddish brown, is normal after whelping. However, if it should change to a putrid-smelling, dark-brown discharge, you should suspect metritis, especially if the bitch's temperature is abnormally high. The condition will usually manifest itself within about twenty-four hours of whelping, and you should consult a vet immediately as it can be fatal. It is normally treated with a course of antibiotics.

Mastitis

It is important to inspect the bitch's teats daily in order check for any signs of this condition, which will cause the teats to become hot, hard and sore. In the event that your bitch shows these symptoms, consult your vet immediately. He will be able to prescribe antibiotics, although the puppies will probably have to be hand-reared while the bitch is being treated (*see* page 174).

Eclampsia

Eclampsia is caused by calcium deficiency in the blood, and is most common in bitches who have had large litters which make enormous demands on her milk supply. A bitch suffering from this condition will become very unsteady on her legs, and will probably twitch or shiver. The symptoms worsen, becoming more dramatic in a very short space of time. The condition is fatal, unless urgent veterinary help is sought. An intravenous injection of calcium will effect an immediate cure, but this must be done quickly.

It is worth ensuring that the bitch is given sufficient calcium supplement during pregnancy, as this may help to prevent eclampsia from occurring (*see* page 161).

Fading Puppy Syndrome

This is a condition where, for no apparent reason, an otherwise healthy puppy, or even litter, goes rapidly into decline. There are various possible causes, which cannot always be identified, but may include hypothermia, trauma, lack of food, infection or parasites. With the improved standards of antenatal and postnatal care, the condition does not appear to manifest itself as often as it did in the past.

Supplementary Feeding and Hand-Rearing

There are a variety of products available for hand-rearing puppies or supplementing feeds. It is wise to consult your vet for his advice on which would be the most suitable in the circumstances.

Supplementary feeding can be done with the aid of a needleless syringe. The puppies will suck the mixture as they become stronger but, if they seem unable to do this, gently squeeze little drops from the syringe directly into their mouths. Be sure not to become overzealous when doing this, for if they should swallow too much too quickly, it may get into their lungs and cause problems that may prove fatal.

Experienced breeders very often know how to 'tube feed' – where a thin tube is inserted down inside the puppy, and the feed squeezed directly into the stomach – but I advise you not to attempt this unless supervised by someone who has great experience of this, for untold damage could be done if it is not tackled correctly. The advantages of this method are that you know exactly how much each puppy is getting (as none can be lost out of the sides of the mouth), and it bypasses the lungs thus preventing any problems from occurring there.

If you are having to hand-rear a litter, either because you have lost the bitch during whelping, so that you have to bring up orphans, or because the bitch has for some reason rejected the puppies, you will have to simulate the mother's cleansing procedure. After feeding, a bitch will clean her puppies with her tongue, the action of which will cause the puppies to urinate and defecate. Until they are about three weeks old, they are unable to relieve themselves without this encouragement. In the absence of the dam, you should do this with some cotton wool dampened with warm water, massaging the area around the genitals and abdomen until they pass something. This should be done after every feed.

You will also have to be especially sure to check that the temperature of the room in which you are rearing the puppies is kept warm and constant. Without the natural warmth created by the bitch's body, there is an even greater risk of hypothermia. In addition, pay particular attention to hygiene, as the risk of infection is higher if puppies have not had the benefit of receiving natural immunity through their mother's milk.

A harlequin bitch with her contented litter.

Care of the Litter

Even when a litter is produced naturally, it is still advisable to request that the vet checks the dam and litter over. In most cases, he will give the dam an injection that will induce her to pass any particles of placenta or other matter that may not have come away with the puppies, and which would eventually set up an infection if left. In the event that an infection develops, the bitch will have a raised temperature, and she will eventually lose interest in nursing her brood. In all probability, her milk will start to go off, thus affecting the health of the puppies also.

All being well, the bitch and her litter should go from strength to strength. For a while afterwards, she may continue to have a vaginal discharge. After the initial green discharge, which is normal after the birth, a dark, reddish discharge will appear. Always keep a close eye on this; in the event of any abnormality, consult the vet. (*See* also page 175.)

Once everything has settled down, and the dam is quite happy with her often demanding brood, be vigilant in surveying the litter and ensure that one or more is not being pushed away from the teats by the strong and more robust of the litter. Sometimes you may find that a smaller or weaker puppy is constantly being pushed out of the general mêlée. This may be for one of two reasons: either it has not received enough sustenance from its mother through being pushed away by its stronger brothers and sisters, or there may be something amiss internally that you would obviously not be able to see. Invariably, you will find that the mother tends not to bother with it, perhaps intuitively knowing that something is not right with this one of her litter. Try to ensure that it is getting its fair share of time on the teats, and that the others do not push it away before it has satisfied itself. If there appears to be no marked improvement over a couple of days, consult your vet. With a large litter, the dam's milk may not be sufficient to sustain them all, so it may be necessary to supplement it with a puppy or baby milk powder (*see* page 174).

Initial Weaning

At approximately eight to ten days, the puppies will be ready to be fed with extra food to help supplement the milk that the dam has been producing. It is at about this time that you will probably notice that their eyes have begun to open.

Every breeder will have his own ideas about weaning, and it is not for me to comment or criticize. I can only tell you how I feed and rear my own Danes. I start supplementing the mother's milk at a very early age, when they are ten days old, or rather when their eyes open. Their first meal consists of a small quantity of finely minced raw best lean beef, warmed in a little hot water, which is always fed at the puppies' blood temperature.

On the first day, feed once, and on the next day twice, morning and night. On the third day feed three times, morning, midday and night. On the fourth day add a sprinkling of bonemeal, and on the fifth day a small quantity of baby cereal mixed with baby milk. Gradually I add honey to the milk meal and soaked wholemeal biscuit to the meat meal. At four weeks of age the puppies are being fed six times a day: three milk feeds and three meat meals. There are a few rare cases of puppies reacting badly to milk, with diarrhoea and sickness. When this occurs I use goats' milk instead of baby milk.

I am also a strong believer in natural yoghurt. If a puppy has had diarrhoea I feed natural live yoghurt to replace the puppy's own normal gut bacterial flora. When a puppy for one reason or another lacks

Daliam Moonbeam. (Photo: Dalton.)

this normal bacterial flora it will be unable to digest milk properly. Live yoghurt contains 'lactobacillus acidophilus' and these bacteria are essential to the digestive system in all dogs and other animals including man. The yoghurt is mixed with a little warm water (again to blood temperature) and vitamin B (which helps the bacteria to settle and multiply).

Remember that your vet should be your closest friend and ally. If you have a good vet you should be able to talk to him about any feeding problems and he should then preventatively advise. Some puppies take to being weaned very quickly and to any of the foods that you now attempt to give them; some, though, are a little slower on the uptake, far preferring the milk that mother provides. It is, of course, very important to try to get the puppies on to solid foods as quickly as possible. The bitch cannot sustain a large demanding brood for long,

'The end result'.

and if they are allowed to keep draining her without your supplementing them, they will eventually cause a loss of condition in the bitch.

So, armed with your moistened minced beef, pick your first puppy
up, always ensuring that your hands are warm, and place a little of the
meat on the puppy's tongue. It can be safely assured that at this stage
the puppy will most likely spit it right back at you; this simply means
that you have to repeat the exercise until it begins to understand that it

178

is in fact supposed to swallow it. At this stage a little meat is quite enough until the puppies get the taste of it and want more.

After about three to four days of teaching them that the meat is in fact good for them, and providing that on the whole they are happy with this, you may start to add some bonemeal to the mince. In these formative days the puppies will need to be fed at least three to four times day.

One week after starting weaning I add milk and cereal to the diet, alternating these with the meals of minced beef. Do not use cows' milk for baby or puppy powdered milk is far more nutritious for the young-sters and least likely to upset their delicate stomachs. I use baby milk powder regularly, mixing one part milk to six parts water and then adding that to baby cereal or rusk, or indeed any cereal that blends smoothly with the milk.

In the early stages of feeding the cereal you may need to use your fingers for the puppies to suck on; it is a far easier way of getting them to accept it. Eventually, as they become easier to wean they will take it happily off a spoon until they are four to five weeks old when they will be eating out of a dish, unaided.

During this weaning period the dam can be taken away for short periods of time which can be gradually extended so that at approxi-mately four weeks of age the puppies will be more interested in the food that you are about to supply them with than in the fact that mother is not with them quite as often as she used to be.

By this time the meals should be increased to up to five or six a day. By the time the puppies are seven or eight weeks old they should be totally weaned away from their mother and eating happily on their own, five times a day.

9

Ailments and Diseases

As you become more involved in the world of dogs, you will learn how important it is to have a veterinary surgeon in whom you have the utmost confidence, and one who will listen to what you say (provided you have years of experience behind you), while he considers the best course of action.

The most well-known diseases are of course distemper, hardpad and leptospirosis together with the modern-day lethal virus, parvo-virus. But apart from being affected internally with viruses and various conditions, a dog can also be troubled by external problems, such as parasites.

Parasites

Parasites can affect dogs either internally or externally. Of the external parasites, the most common and well-known is, of course, the flea.

Fleas

Whenever you buy a puppy or a dog, always check or have your vet check to ensure that there are no signs of any fleas being present on your dog. The most obvious sign that a dog has fleas is the presence of flea droppings which usually occur along the back, near the tail and around the neck. These droppings resemble small particles of dark grit and should never be ignored.

The female flea lays her eggs in the dog's environment – the basket and bedding, the carpet, soft furnishings, or in any other warm place where they can hatch out undisturbed. The females are usually slightly lighter in colour than the males and very often appear to be larger and slightly less acrobatic, for a male flea can leap up to approx-imately sixty feet (18m) in the air.

Fleas are most usually to be found at the base of the tail and, slightly less commonly, behind the ears. If you cannot see any fleas moving

Ch. Endroma Morgans Boy. (Photo: Pearce.)

about in the coat, but your dog is scratching himself, start looking for the tell-tale signs of droppings. If you do discover these, place your dog on an old white sheet and spray him with an appropriate aerosol parasiticide for use on dogs, or a good flea powder. Always take great care to protect the eyes and nose of the dog. Within a few moments the fleas will start to leave the body of their host and you will see them on the white sheet. Repeat this procedure as instructed on the container of the flea spray/powder and once again watch to see if any fall on to the white sheet.

As soon as the presence of fleas is detected, always take immediate action to rid your dog of the irritation they are causing him. Always be sure to adhere to the instructions given on the treatment container, especially with regard to carrying out the second treatment (which is needed to eradicate any fleas that have hatched since the first treatment). Another obvious flea deterrent and cure is bathing in a good-quality parasiticidal shampoo for dogs. Such preparations are available from good pet shops and also from your vet.

When treating the dog, it is important to treat his environment as

Ch. Czarina v.t. Buitengeburen of Impton. (Photo: A.R.W.)

well: the dog's quarters should be scrubbed out and the bedding treated or destroyed. Treat the area around the basket and anywhere else to which the dog has any access, paying special attention to any small cracks in the floor, his basket, and any furnishings where eggs may be nestling. Vacuum cleaning the carpet regularly helps to remove eggs, but is not a cure in itself. Always be sure to empty the vacuum bag straight into the dustbin or incinerator when you have finished.

Fleas can cause an allergic reaction in animals, causing skin problems (which have to be treated separately) and general debility, and they are also the intermediate host of the tapeworm (*see* page 185), so it is important to deal with them quickly and efficiently. Many owners are extremely sensitive to the suggestion that their dog may have fleas; they frequently refuse to believe it and so do nothing about it. Fleas are extremely common, and the vast majority of dogs will pick them up at some time in their lives, whether or not they live in a clean environment. It is cruel not to treat a dog who has fleas, and no owner should feel embarrassed about having to eradicate these pests when the odd occassion arises.

Lice

Lice are not as common as fleas but if they should attach themselves to a dog, they can cause a great deal of distress. They are also very hard to eliminate and need rigorous and careful attention for their rate of reproduction is quite frightening. Regular bathing in a shampoo recommended by your veterinary surgeon is recommended with treatment being given at the specified intervals to eradicate this nuisance. Lice spend their entire lifecycle on the hosts, so there should be no need to treat the dog's environment. You must, however, treat any other dogs with whom the infested dog has come into contact.

Ticks

Ticks, again, are not quite so common as the flea and are usually found in rural areas. Cattle are the main carriers of ticks, and so ticks are usually picked up during a walk in the countryside.

Once attached to a dog, the tick will appear to be a greyish or beige small lump, with the head completely obscured from vision. You need to be very careful when ridding a dog of a tick because it is extremely important that the part buried in the dog's skin is destroyed. If left behind, it can quickly cause infection. For this reason, do not attempt to remove a tick without first bathing it in a suitable acaridide solution, recommended by your vet, which will cause the tick to release its grip. You can then pull it off with a pair of tweezers.

Ear Mites

These microscopic parasites can cause immense irritation to your dog, causing him to scratch his ears constantly and rub his head against the floor or furniture. An early warning sign is a discharge of a dark sticky, waxy substance from the ear. Seek the assistance of your vet who will take a scraping of the substance for analysis and prescribe the appropriate treatment.

Mange

Mange is a skin complaint caused by mites and, whilst the condition is not seen that often, it can cause a lot of suffering to the dog and immense worry to the owner in trying to cure it.

There are basically two types of mange: sarcoptic and demodectic, each caused by a different mite, and each necessitating immediate expert attention.

Sarcoptic Mange
This causes severe irritation to the skin, most commonly around the muzzle, ears, legs and belly, and you will need the advice of your vet to deal with it. He will in most cases take a scraping from the skin for analysis so that the diagnosis can be confirmed and a course of treatment prescribed. Sarcoptic mange is extremely infectious, so affected dogs must be isolated from other animals, and all bedding and kennelling should be washed in a suitable parasiticide recommended by the vet. In severe cases, it will cause thickening of the skin, scurfiness, loss of weight and depression. It can also cause irritation to human skin, although this can be remedied with treatment.

Demodectic Mange
This form of mange is less common than sarcoptic mange, and is seen most often in very young dogs. It is not contagious and does not cause irritation until the condition has become quite severe. Severe infection will also cause depression, extensive hair loss, and thickening of the skin, which will become greasy and have an unpleasant smell. It is a more serious problem than sarcoptic mange in that it can rarely be treated successfully; it does not seem to respond positively to treatment and usually reappears just when you think it has been conquered. The progression of the infection is heartbreaking to watch and, in many cases, only euthanasia can end the dog's suffering.

Harvest Mites

These can be another cause of irritation to the dog and can be quite difficult to detect. They are red in colour but are only just visible to the human eye. They primarily affect the feet, legs and belly of the dog. Bathing in a suitable shampoo is necessary, with particular attention being paid to these areas.

Worms

In this day and age of medical science, there is no reason for a dog to have worms, for there are plenty of preparations available to prevent infestation occurring. However, there are two types of worm most likely to affect dogs: tapeworms and roundworms.

Int. and Nord. Ch. Harmony Hill Lied of Airways. (Photo: Andreas.)

Tapeworms

The tapeworm lives in the intestine of the dog. As the worm grows, segments of the worm break off and are passed out of the body to appear around the anus or on the dog's faeces. These segments, which contain the tapeworm's eggs, look like grains of rice and are easily noticeable to the vigilant owner. Other symptoms may include general listlessness and a deterioration in coat condition.

Tapeworm eggs are passed indirectly from dog to dog via the flea, which ingests the eggs when they are passed out into the environment. A dog can then become infected by eating the flea, which often happens when the dog bites at himself to relieve irritation caused by fleas. This is one of the reasons that flea control is very important.

There are effective preparations for eradicating worms, but all dogs should be wormed regularly to prevent infestation occurring in the first place. Treatment in tablet or paste form is readily available, and your vet will be able to advise you on the necessary dosage and the frequency with which to administer it.

Roundworms

The *Toxocara canis* roundworm is the one that most commonly affects dogs, usually puppies. They live in the small intestine and are eventually passed out of the body where they can easily be seen in the faeces, and occasionally in the vomit. At the same time, eggs are passed out of the body, but these are invisible to the naked eye. After about three weeks, the eggs develop into larvae, and it is at this stage that they are highly infectious, not only to puppies but to humans, children in particular, in whom the larvae can cause loss of eyesight if they manage to reach the optic nerve. This is extremely rare since eggs are not infectious until they develop into larvae at around three weeks after they have been passed by the dog, and any larvae that are ingested are usually killed by the stomach acids. Nevertheless, the risk does exist, which is one of the reasons for many of today's parks and commons being closed to dogs, and confirms the importance of regular worming, and of clearing up after your dog, especially in public places.

Apart from the appearance of worms in the faeces, other signs that a puppy may have worms include lack of condition and general dullness, a pot-bellied appearance (which should not be confused with the rounded tummy of a healthy, well-fed puppy), and sometimes an intermittent, retching cough.

Owing to the complicated lifecycle of the *Toxocara canis* roundworm, most puppies are born already infected with it, which is why it is extremely important to worm puppies properly. Most puppies will have to be wormed more than once during their first few weeks, and regularly throughout their adult lives. Your vet will be able to advise you on the appropriate preparation, the necessary dosage and the frequency of treatment.

Gastric Dilation or Bloat

Every Great Dane owner dreads this condition rearing its ugly head for unless immediate action is taken the results are usually fatal. Basically it is caused by internal body gasses releasing into the stomach, causing the stomach to harden and distend. The result is immense pain to the poor dog and care should always be taken to keep an eye open for any discomfort being shown by the dog in this area. The

Danelagh Eloise of Walkmyll. (Photo: Pearce.)

condition can be further complicated if the dilated stomach twists, causing gastric torsion. At this stage, the condition is fatal, so if you suspect that your dog may have bloat, immediate veterinary assistance must be sought.

Distemper

Distemper is probably one of the most known diseases amongst canine and non-canine factions. In the days of yesteryear it was one of the most virulent killers of many dogs before a suitable preventative vaccine against it was found.

Nowadays, although it is still as lethal as ever and there are still occasional outbreaks of it, vaccination has meant that it is simple to control. Vaccination is done while the puppy is still young, at around ten to twelve weeks of age, at the same time as he is immunized against the other possible killer diseases that could affect him.

The initial signs of this disease being present include a high temperature which is followed by a cough and a thick, yellow mucous discharge from the eyes and nose. The dog appears to be generally out of sorts. The cough will worsen and be followed by vomiting and loss of control of the bowels. In the latter stages of this disease the dog's central nervous system becomes affected which causes the dog to start having convulsions and fits. Eventually, to bring the dog's suffering to an end, euthanasia may be the only solution.

Even with the protection of inoculations it has been known for a dog to contract the disease, but immunisation prevents the disease from developing.

Hard Pad

Hard pad is a widely known term and condition, which invariably accompanies the preceding disease in its latter stages. It is as it sounds, a swelling and hardening of the dog's feet and pads, which make it extremely painful for the dog to walk. This of course should not be confused with interdigital cysts.

Leptospirosis

There are two forms of this disease, both of which can be inoculated against, once again at the time of the puppy's primary injections. Before suitable protection was found to guard dogs against this virulent disease, it was the scourge of kennels throughout the land; many kennels were virtually wiped out because it is so highly contagious and easily transmitted. Its symptoms may appear to be similar to several other conditions that are also inoculated against.

Leptospira ictoerohaemorrhagiae attacks the liver, and is carried and transmitted by rats and other dogs through their urine. People who live in country areas should always be particularly careful where their dogs drink from, although with large colonies of rats in towns as well, care should always be taken anyway. Never let your dog drink water from a puddle if at all possible, for one can never be sure that a rat has not urinated in that water. And never leave your dog's water bowl outside at night with water in it. Empty it and place it out of harm's way. In the morning, ensure that he has fresh water outside if that is what he is used to. This, of course, is especially important for dogs who live in kennels.

The onset of the disease is sudden, and the symptoms are lack of appetite, sudden rise in temperature, jaundice (which shows in yellowing of the eyes, gums and skin), insatiable thirst, accompanied by vomiting and diarrhoea. This may be followed by the appearance of haemorrhages in the eye, and conjunctivitis may develop.

Leptospira canicola is the other form of the disease. This form attacks the kidneys and is more prevalent in town dogs. As with the first form of leptospirosis, the disease is transmitted through infected urine, but the onset of the illness is not so sudden and the symptoms are slightly different. General dullness and slight indifference to food is followed by depression, total loss of appetite, excess thirst and urination, vomiting and abdominal pain in the kidney region. In severe cases, mouth ulcers and halitosis may develop as a result of damage to the kidneys.

Both forms of leptospirosis are usually fatal, and both forms can be transmitted to humans. So if a dog contracts this disease, the utmost care must be taken whilst nursing him. Obviously, expert care and attention is required from your veterinary surgeon.

Parvovirus

This is the modern-day scourge of the dog world which first made its appearance in 1978, although science has now found a vaccine to protect dogs against it. One form of this disease attacks the heart muscles, usually of young puppies, the other attacks the intestine. The latter type is more commonly seen, and causes severe vomiting, depression, anorexia, and foul-smelling diarrhoea which often contains blood. It is an ugly and painful disease which attacks the weakest animals – usually puppies, but sometimes old dogs – with quick and, in the vast majority of cases, fatal results.

The disease is usually contracted via infected faeces. It is extremely infectious and will wipe out an entire kennel because of the difficulty in eradicating it from the environment. Vaccines are effective but puppies will usually have to have two vaccinations a few weeks apart to ensure total protection.

Canine distemper (hard pad), infectious canine hepatitis, leptospirosis and canine parvovirus are usually vaccinated against at the same time, with a combined vaccine. You will see that this combined vaccine is referred to as DHLP on the certificate of vaccination that is issued by your vet on completion of the course. Your vet will recommend regular boostering. If the mother of a litter has been regularly boostered she will pass immunity to her offspring through her milk. This, it is generally thought, gives them protection to around six weeks of age when the time is near for them to receive their own course of immunization.

Kennel Cough

With care and attention this is not an extremely dangerous complaint, but if the initial symptoms are ignored, it can turn into something more worrying. It is quickly spread from dog to dog, as it is easily contracted, and results in the dog developing a rasping and worrying cough. If detected quickly it can be treated and then follows a period of recuperation and isolation. For dogs who attend many shows and who spend any time in boarding kennels, there is a vaccination against it.

There are different types of kennel cough, each caused by a different virus. *Bordetella bronchiseptica* is a bacterial infection causing lethargy and loss of appetite, and can eventually lead to pneumonia when death can occur. The vaccine against this comes in the form of nose drops, and will last for about six months. The other virus most often associated with kennel cough is *Canine parainfluenza*. Vaccination against this can be included in the normal booster vaccinations given each year.

Isolation

If you have several dogs and one should contract any of the above illnesses it is always advisable to keep the ailing animal away from others for as long as necessary. With a large kennel, you can set aside an area for just this purpose. If, however, you keep dogs in the house, it does make life more difficult but it is not impossible to keep the disease confined provided adequate precautions are taken.

Try to establish a 'no-go' area between the room where the sick animal is recovering and the area or rooms occupied by his friends. Whenever it is necessary to go into the room to care for the sick animal, the following rules can help to stop the spread of infection.

If possible, one person should have sole charge of caring for the sick animal. On leaving the room, the carer should change his clothes. Always have an antiseptic spray at the door of the room so that hands and feet can be quickly sprayed before coming into contact with the other dogs of the household. Be sure to wash your hands as soon as possible after attending to the sick animal.

Austral. Ch. Impton Eagle. (Photo: Trafford.)

If you are an avid showgoer, you will know that when entering a show, on the bottom of the entry form, you sign a declaration. This states that you agree to abide by the rules of the Kennel Club and demands that if you have a dog or have been in contact with dogs that are suffering from any contagious diseases you will not attend a show for a period of six weeks. Any one who genuinely cares for dogs whether they be his own or other people's will have no qualms about giving up a few weeks of pleasure for the safety of others. Unfortunately there are a few people in the world who are completely selfish and have no care or second thoughts for others and will continue to show while having a sick animal at home. It is worth reiterating here that showing should be kept in perspective. It is never worth risking the spread of disease, whatever the prize.

Diarrhoea

This is a very unpleasant condition for the animal that is suffering from it, but with care and common sense, it can be quickly cleared up. This is one of the main reasons that when buying your puppy from the breeder of your choice, you should strictly adhere to the diet sheet that you are given. This is given to ensure the well-being of the puppy and will recommend foods that he is used to receiving without suffering any ill effects. Be warned that any deviation from this will quickly upset the puppy's tummy resulting in a severe cases of the 'runs'. If not treated immediately, it will quickly cause dehydration and debilitate the puppy very quickly.

Of course, diarrhoea is not confined just to puppies; adult dogs can suffer from it too, sometimes for no apparent reason, although diet is usually the cause. They may have foraged in the garden or park, and managed to find some unwholesome titbit to eat. Any change in diet should be made very gradually and for good reason.

Diarrhoea can be treated by your vet with medication. If your dog seems prone to the complaint, your veterinary surgeon may suggest that you keep medication at hand to give when necessary.

Diarrhoea can be a symptom of gastro-enteritis and is also one of the main symptoms of parvovirus. Diarrhoea often accompanies other diseases. In cases such as these, there is usually a presence of blood and, in parvovirus, this can be quite evident. So it is worth investigation for other symptoms. If, however, the diarrhoea is a result of dietary change or a mild form of gastro-enteritis, your veterinary surgeon will recommend that the dog is not allowed any food for at least twelve hours. He will usually advise that the dog should be given boiled water, a little at a time, sometimes with lectade powder dissolved in it. This will counteract any possibility of dehydration. When he is allowed to eat, he should be given small quantities of light food, such as chicken or fish mixed with boiled rice, which will need to be given as instructed by the vet.

Eczema

Eczema is inflammation of the skin caused by excessive licking and scratching. It usually appears in patches and can be wet or dry. The initial irritation causing the dog to scratch can be caused by too much protein (especially offal) in the diet, while in other cases, the irritation may be produced by allergy, such as that which may result from flea infestation.

The hair on the affected area should be clipped away and the skin cleaned. In most cases of wet eczema, the area should be left exposed to the air rather than covered up. If a cause such as flea allergy can be identified, the dog should also be treated to eradicate fleas, although this should be done with the advice of your vet. Antibiotics are usually required to clear up the condition, and anti-inflammatory medicines to reduce the irritation may also be prescribed. With all cases of eczema, a visit to the vet is necessary before the condition becomes too advanced.

Cysts

These can appear on the body or on the dog's feet between the toes. The latter are known as interdigital cysts, the former as serbaceous cysts.

A cyst appears initially as a small swelling or lump which will increase in size as time goes on. Eventually this may erupt and an evil-smelling pus will be discharged. Interdigital cysts are usually quite painful to the dog as they appear as a swelling between the dog's toes, causing lameness. Your veterinary surgeon will need to be consulted in case a course of antibiotics is necessary. In some cases, minor surgery may be needed to remove them.

Pyometra

This is a condition which affects only bitches since it is a disease of the uterus. There are two types of pyometra: open and closed, the latter being far harder to detect because the symptoms are less obvious. Both forms will cause abdominal tensions, loss of appetite, excessive thirst and a high temperature. With open pyometra, the surest sign is the appearance of a dark brown, highly noxious discharge from the vulva. Closed pyometra is so called because there is no leakage of pus from the vulva; instead it is retained within the uterus.

The condition usually becomes apparent within a few weeks of the bitch having been in season, and it is more likely to affect bitches who have not been bred from, although there is no hard and fast rule governing this.

With both forms of this condition, urgent veterinary assistance is needed for, if ignored, it is fatal. Sometimes medication is advised but in the vast majority of cases, a hysterectomy is carried out.

General First Aid

Bites

By bites I am referring to bites caused by other dogs, for instance during a fight. Usually they are deep tears of skin where the teeth of the other dog have penetrated.

In cases such as this it is always advisable for your vet to inspect the damage for often a course of antibiotics is necessary to stop any infection setting into the wound. Depending on the instructions given by the vet it will usually be necessary to cleanse the wound daily with a mild antiseptic lotion before suitable medication is administered.

Burns

If your pet should get burnt, either by fire or hot water, it is necessary to act quickly, as it is with humans. Immediately drench the burnt area with cold water, which, if the burn is not too severe, will prevent further skin tissue being affected. If the burn is minor, the skin may simply redden, but if it is any more serious, consult your veterinary surgeon who will need to see the dog as quickly as possible. As with other accidents, shock may occur (*see* page 195).

Choking

This can come on suddenly and may be caused by a foreign object being stuck at the back of the dog's throat. There may not be time to get the dog to the vet, so you may have to deal with this yourself. Quickly open the dog's mouth and look for any signs of obstruction. Sometimes a piece of bone may be stuck and can be quickly released but be very careful not to push the object further down the throat. If you cannot remove the object, it is a case of emergency and your vet will need to see the dog as quickly as possible. Choking can also be caused by a dog swallowing a wasp or bee (*see* page 196).

Poisoning

There are several poisonous agents that your dog may have the misfortune to come into contact with, which can easily be picked up by accident. For instance, slug bait, or weed killers such as Paraquat that may be used in public places, for example on road verges, are easily come across. With this particular type of poison, the dog does not even have to eat it for simply inhaling the fumes can cause serious internal damage. Rat poison that may be inadvertently found by your dog can cause haemorrhaging prior to death.

Always be on your guard for these toxins. If your dog should pick up some poison, and has been seen doing so, it is very important to make the dog sick. In order to do this, force the dog to drink a salt solution as quickly as possible, and copious amounts of water. If the poison is known to be a corrosive type, substitute the salt water for milk, and do not try to make the dog sick.

As soon as possible, get the dog to the veterinary surgery so that immediate assistance can be sought. Always remember to take the details of the poison with you, if known, as this can be a help to the vet in deciding a course of emergency treatment.

Heat stroke

The most common cause of heat stroke is leaving a dog shut in a car during warm weather. Even with ventilation, the temperature inside a car on a hot summer's day can soar, causing any dog severe distress within minutes.

Heat stroke is a serious emergency and is fatal if it is not dealt with in time. The symptoms include excessive panting, collapse and a very high temperature. Remove the dog from the car and douse him immediately with cold water. Give him copious amounts of water to drink (with a little salt added, if possible), after which he should be kept calm and cool and taken straight to the vet. He will probably need to be treated for shock (*see* below).

It is far better to avoid the situation in the first place: never leave a dog shut in a car on a warm day; and in cooler weather, leave the windows open and fit grilles.

Shock

This can occur after any traumatic experience, most commonly after a road accident. Usually the dog will collapse or be in a state of semi-consciousness. Very often the gums and eyelids will pale. Usually the dog will feel cold especially in his legs and feet, and breathing will often be rapid and shallow. It is extremely important to ensure that the dog is kept warm and quiet until you can get help, so quickly cover him with a blanket or something similar. Keep the dog's head lower than the rest of the body and ensure that the airway is clear. If breathing appears to have stopped, blow down the muzzle at the rate of twenty times a minute. If the heart stops, lay the dog on his side and press the chest at the rate of sixty times a minute.

Stings

When summer is at its height, there comes the menace of bees and wasps. How inviting these flying objects are to any playful dog. Of course, the danger with wasps and bees are that they can inflict a sting which, apart from being extremely painful, can be lethal if deposited in the throat. Obviously, urgent medical assistance is needed before the swelling in the throat proves fatal.

It is always advisable to have in your medical box anti-histamine tablets for emergencies like this. You are usually able to obtain them from your veterinary surgeon, but alternatively Piriton tablets can be bought from any major chemist. Before rushing your dog to the vet, quickly administer the anti-histamine.

If, however, the sting is on the dog's body, it is usually painful but in the majority of cases will not prove to be lethal unless the dog is allergic to stings.

Wasps always withdraw their stings but a bee may leave its sting behind. This can be removed with a pair of tweezers. Whether or not this has been accomplished, the area should be swabbed with a solution of bicarbonate of soda to relieve the discomfort. For a wasp sting, apply vinegar or lemon juice.

Administering Medicine

When the vet has seen the patient, he will in some cases prescribe a course of treatment depending on the nature of the illness or injury. Whatever drugs are prescribed, it is essential that they are administered as advised. Sometimes they will come in liquid form, sometimes in tablet form.

Some dogs take medicines quite easily, for instance a liquid medication can be given by pouring it over the dog's food. However, depending on his illness, he may have a loss of appetite, in which case you will have to administer the drug directly. One of the simplest ways to administer liquid medications is with a needleless syringe. With the prescribed amount in it, simply squirt it slowly into the dog's mouth as

Adminstering a tablet orally.

far back as possible without making him choke. Tablets can be a little harder to give, although if the dog is feeling hungry, it can be disguised in one of his favourite tit-bits. But if he will not take it like this, you will have to do it the hard way.

Hold the dog's head up, but not too high, and make him open his mouth. Push the tablet as far down his throat as possible, then quickly close his mouth, ensuring that it stays shut whilst you massage his throat gently in order to make him swallow. If done efficiently and quickly, this will not be a traumatic experience for either you or your dog.

Care of the Teeth

Although teeth care does not come under the umbrella of ailments, unless your dog's teeth are properly cared for complications can set in and upset the dog's health.

One of the commonest causes of trouble is a steady build up of tar-tar, which if allowed to become embedded in between the teeth, can

Cleaning the teeth.

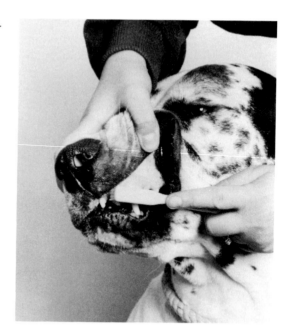

set up infections within the gums. This will eventually lead to the loss of teeth and bad breath.

Several leading manufacturers now produce a doggy toothpaste and you literally clean your dog's teeth in a similar fashion to your own, using a soft-bristle brush or cloth. If this is done regularly the chances of any dental problems occurring are lessened and go towards allowing your dog to enjoy a good, healthy constitution.

Old Age

While old age affects almost all living creatures eventually, in the canine world it seems to come around so quickly. One minute the love of your life is a fun-loving, mischievous gamboling puppy, but then it hardly seems any time at all before he is finding it that much more difficult to get up when lying down, and then may come the time when he starts to have the odd accident in the house because he is unable to control himself in time to go out into the garden.

To make his old age that much more comfortable, always ensure that his bed and blankets are in a cosy place out of any draughts. Make sure that he has plenty of opportunity to go outside to relieve himself and do not be tempted to scold him when perhaps the odd mistake does occur, for as a model house-trained dog he will already be upset at this slip.

As with humans, old age causes the body to start slowing down and you will probably find that he tends to sleep a lot more in the autumn of his life. Some parts of the body may start to slow down and show signs of deterioration but with veterinary care these can be helped with the use of certain drugs and medication to help lengthen the dog's life.

Whilst your dog is enjoying life and does not seem to be in any apparent pain, apart from perhaps a little mild arthritis, and appears to be sustaining a reasonable appetite, he will lead a happy and fulfilling life. But when certain organs or areas of the body start to show the more serious effects of age, he may not have that zest for life that he has enjoyed up until then and may show signs of suffering.

Euthanasia

When your dog shows signs of suffering, the time has probably come for you to be guided by the advice of the professional who has tended him through his years from puppyhood to eventual adulthood, and that person may now advise that it is kinder to put him to sleep in order to save him from any further suffering.

It is not uncommon for any owner to want to avoid this moment, however obvious it is that it must be carried out. It is only natural to shy away from making a decision that will part you from your faithful and devoted companion. But remember always that, because he has been with you through good and bad, accepting your every mood and whim quite happily, you now owe it to him to protect him from any suffering, thinking not of yourself but of him. That special relationship can never be taken away, it is an invisible link that has existed between every owner and his canine friend through time immemorial. By making that most difficult decision you are giving him the chance to leave this world peacefully, and that in itself is the act of a true and devoted companion and friend.

10

Famous Kennels, Past and Present

In Chapter 1 we saw the evolvement of the breed throughout the ages up until the First World War when the breed suffered greatly, both in the United Kingdom and Germany, because of the terrible conditions the war brought to Europe. After this the Great Dane began to recover both here and on the Continent. In Germany, the UK and the United States, dedicated breeders sought to bring their breed back into prominence and it must be said that their efforts were certainly rewarded.

The breeders in Germany faced their enormous task of resurrecting the breed with Germanic precision and thoroughness. They ruled that stud-dogs must be over twenty months of age before they could be allowed to mate bitches. Brood-bitches had to be over eighteen months of age before this could happen, and if they were under twenty months it was only permitted for them to rear a maximum of four puppies. If, however, they were over twenty months this was extended to six puppies. They also decreed that brood-bitches were allowed to have only one litter in twelve months.

In the UK, two kennels stand out from all others in the history of the breed this century, having become household names among Dane fanciers, and they are the Ouborough and Send kennels. These were started when two gentlemen, J.V. Rank and Gordon Stewart, devoted their time, energies and vast fortunes on the breed. Many beautiful specimens were imported into the country, mainly from Germany. The actual number recorded as being imported by the two millionaires was, in fact, eighty-six between the First and Second World Wars.

During this periods, these kennels started to produce top-winning and superb stock. One of them was also to give the dog world one of its most well-known judges, unfortunately no longer with us. He was Bill Siggers who started off his distinguished career as Kennel Manager for the Ouboroughs.

Although Mr Rank had imported several dogs during the earlier part of the century it was not until the mid 1920s that his counterpart brought his newly acquired Great Danes into the country. One can imagine the competition that these two massive kennels must have created during this time, each producing beautiful specimens. The show ring in those days was completely dominated by their presence. Both kennels kept large numbers of dogs and it is reported that at one time the Send Kennels of Mr Stewart had over two hundred Great Danes!

Probably one of the best-known Danes to have entered the country after the First World War was a dog, Valthari of Bellary (imported by a Miss Callinder), who had the distinction of being unbeaten in the show ring in his native Germany.

Unlike today, the English Kennel Club did not have their 'Change of Name' ruling, which meant that a dog could be transferred from one owner to another and the entire name could be changed. (Nowadays, of course, this is not allowed, and one is able to add only a kennel name provided that the dog or bitch has not qualified to be entered in the Kennel Club's Stud Book.) One such case was a bitch that Bill Siggers owned named Viola. She was the result of Rufflyn breeding, another well-known kennel at around this time belonging to Mr Coates. Viola was transferred to Mr Rank from her owner, re-emerging under a new identity, Lisa of Ouborough and making her name by winning several CCs for her owner.

Ch. Primley Pericles has to be classed amongst Danedom's 'greats'. Bred by Mr Whitney, who had bred with great success over the years, he joined the Ouboroughs in 1925 at two years of age. One of his progeny was another famous Dane, Ch. Vivien of Ouborough.

During the 1920s a definite pattern emerged, with the greatest competition arising between the two top kennels of Send and Ouborough, although the Sends did not, in fact, win their first CC until 1926, that being with Brenda of Send. From that year on, the battle noticeably hotted up, with the Ouboroughs winning fifteen CCs in 1927. In 1929, the gap between the two kennels was narrowing, just one CC between them, the Ouboroughs just having the advantage.

A distinct turn-around came in 1930 when the Send Great Danes had eighteen CCs to their credit to the Ouborough's four. In 1931 the Send kennels were still in the lead but with a fewer number of CCs, fourteen to nine. By 1932 the Ouboroughs once again had taken up the lead, having won twelve CCs to their rival's four, and 1933 was equally successful for them, gaining one more ticket than the preceding year with the Send's total being reduced to three. This pattern continued, with the Ouboroughs in the ascendancy until in 1936 there were no CCs won by the Send kennel.

While the Sends and the Ouboroughs were dominating the scene in the UK, in Germany in the 1920s the Saalburg kennels were beginning to come to the fore. Their owner was Karl Farber, who was especially famous for his great stud-dog, Ch. Dolf v.d. Saalburg. He was the result of Ch. Bosco v.d. Saalburg out of his own bitch Fauna Monguntia who was sired by another German star, Ch. Famulus Hansa. The Saalburgs produced many beautiful animals, including the famous Ch. Ferguni v. Loheland, and World Ch. Kalandus v. Drachenstein.

America was also making great advances with its stock in the 1920s. Much of the strength in the American breeding programmes, as with the UK, came from Germany and by the 1930s the Walnut kennels began to make their mark. Two of the most famous were little sisters, Ch. Fionne v. Loheland and Ch. Ferguni v. Loheland of Walnut Hall.

Another American kennel that was known at this time was Brae Tarn owned by Mr R. Stevens whose eight Champions included six imports. Three of these were Ch. Nero Hexengold, Ch. Randolph Hexengold (his son), and Ch. Czardus v. Eppelin Spring-Norris who sired ten Champions during his illustrious life. Two of these were Ch. Heide of Brae Tarn and Ch. Jansen of Brae Tarn. It is widely acknowledged that the Brae Tarns have helped form the basis of Great Dane breeding in America as it is known today.

Another outstanding dog imported from Germany was Ch. Zorn v. Birkenhof who arrived in the USA after an outstanding career in Germany, including being BIS at the German Sieger Show in 1936. Another Dane important in the formation of the breed was Ch. Kuno v. Freigericht and Ch. Steinbachers King. The result of a match between Ch. Bosco v.d. Saalburg and Fauna Moguntia (which had produced Ch. Dolf v.d. Saalburg) was Ger. Ch. Etfa v. Saalburg. After considerable success in Germany, she went on to great things in the USA for her new owner Joseph Eigenbauer. She was Best of Breed at the great Westminster Show and produced eight Champion progeny. Her pedigree is still behind many of the pedigrees of today's winning Great Danes in America.

Ch. Ador Tipp Topp must not be forgotten in the breed's history of the earlier part of this century, for this harlequin won the Westminster Show in 1924.

Returning to the UK, although it would appear that all the winning was done by the two top kennels of Send and Ouborough, there were still some other very successful and dedicated breeders showing and improving the stock of that time. Several kennels also emerged from the stock of these two successful and dynamic kennels. The Blendons of Muriel Osborne, for instance, was founded on these two lines; she bred her first Champion in 1930.

In 1931, Mr and Mrs Rank crossed the Atlantic to exhibit at the Westminster Show with their Faun of Ouborough and Rhena v.d. Rheinschange. The dogs both remained in the USA after this show with new owners where they soon gained their American titles.

During the Second World War, the breeding of Great Danes again suffered a reversal and when peace reigned once more in the mid-1940s, two kennels emerged in Great Britain to take up the challenge again: the Blendons of Miss Osborne and the Ouboroughs. It was the Ouboroughs who had the distinction of making up the second Champion in post-war years – Ch. Royalism of Ouborough. Such was the success of the breeding programme of the Ouboroughs that the success that they had enjoyed in the 1930s continued on into the 1940s both through their wins in the show ring and through the progeny of their stud-dogs.

The peak of their career came in the shape of the Great Dane Ch. Elch Edler of Ouborough who was to go on to do what no other Great Dane has yet, to date, been able to match – Best in show at Crufts. Born in 1951, a son of Kalandus of Ouborough and Ch. Raet of Ouborough, he was bred by Mr Rank who, after all he had achieved with his beloved breed, failed to live to see the day that is the fulfilment of every breeder's dream. This win came after a highly successful show career which had begun in the ascendancy virtually as soon as he entered the show ring as a puppy. In fact, he gained his title in three straight shows while he was still being shown in the Puppy classes. Bill Siggers was by Elch Edlers's side as he piloted him to the winner's rostrum on that unforgettable day.

Many breeders who had been active prior to the Second World War did not reappear after hostilities had ended. However, others slowly began to take an interest in our lovely breed and took up the challenge of resurrecting it, for the second time this century. The Winome Great Danes of Mrs Rowbery started at around this time, and her Ch. Juan of Winome was the first Champion to be made up in the breed after the war.

In 1948, Gladys Clayton made up Ch. Bon Adventure of Barvae. A daughter of Rebellion of Ouborough and born during the war, she was the first bitch Champion to gain her title after the war. Apart from enjoying considerable success with this breed, Mrs Clayton together with her daughter Pat went on to become highly respected and established breeders of Beagles and Miniature Pinschers also.

One of the prominent harlequin kennels of that time came in the shape of the Wideskies Great Danes owned by Miss Lomas. She has been predominant in this colour for many years, both before and after the war. Her first Champion, Ch. Cloud of Wideskies, was made up in 1952.

The Ickford Great Danes were owned by Mrs S. Laming. By mating Radiance of Ladymead to Ch. Royalism of Ouborough, the breed was given Ch. Dawnlight of Ickford, Int. Ch. Anndale Moonlight of Ickford and Int. Ch. Anndale Royalight of Ickford.

During the 1940s, the Bringtonhill kennel of Mrs Ennals was formed and it was in 1950 that her first Champion was made up, a fawn bitch named Basra of Bringtonhill. In the same year, another Champion was made up for this kennel, this time a black, Ch. Banshee of Bringtonhill. Six Champions gained their titles from this kennel in all, four of them being fawn and two black.

One of the oldest kennels was begun by Mrs C. Russell whose Oldmanor prefix was created in 1938. Along with her daughter Olive, she bred the brindle bitch who in 1953 was to become Ch. Imogen of Oldmanor. Ch. Moyalism of Winome was her sire while her dam was Dainty of Oldmanor. Their Ch. Oldmanor Pioneer of Daneii was the sire of thirteen UK Champions, with his stock winning ninety Challenge Certificates in all. The bloodlines of this kennel were centred on Ouborough breeding, then incorporating Winome, Blendon and Moonsfield into it. Olive married the Reverend Davis who shared the same enthusiasm for the breed that mother and daughter enjoyed. Sixteen Champions were bred by the Oldmanors and their bloodlines still exist, continuing to enrich the world of Great Danes to this present day.

For the Moonsfield kennels of Mrs E. Harrild, 1953 was also a year to remember: Tandye of Moonsfield gained her title, making this the first Champion for the kennel. She was a daughter of Ch. Royalism of Ouborough out of Tango of Moonsfield.

As with the previous three decades, the Ouboroughs were still very much in evidence, making two Champions up in 1952, Ch. Relate of Ouborough and Ch. Rhagodia of Ouborough; 1953 saw Elch Edler, of course, have a triumphant year while Ch. Vegar of Ouborough won her title for her owner Mrs I.B. Jones. In 1954 a dog who was bred similarly to Elch Edler from an earlier litter won his Champion's crown, Ch. Festival of Ouborough.

Clausentum is a name that is known throughout the world of Great

Ch. Oldmanor Pioneer of Daneii.

Danes and in 1956 the mother and daughter partnership of Mrs H.A. and Miss J. Lanning made up their first Champion. This was a home-bred male, Ch. Challenger of Clausentum, who was by Ch. Bronx of Blendon out of Claire of Clausentum. They were no strangers to the world of dogs for their prefix had been originally registered in 1944 and their successful bloodlines are based on the combination of Ouborough and Blendon stock. Their dedication and knowledge brought to the world of Great Danes Ch. Fergus of Clausentum, who has to be acknowledged as amongst the greats of the dog world.

Several stud-dogs of major importance have emerged in this breed in post-war years, but first and foremost of these must be Ch. Fergus of Clausentum. Fergus is behind most of the top-winning kennels of

Ch. Fergus of Clausentum.

today. Born in 1967, he was sired by Clausentum Danelaghs Quillan out of Creole of Clausentum.

Quillan was imported from the USA and bred by Miss Nancy Carroll-Draper. Quillan's grandfather appears on both sides of his pedigree, namely Ch. Dinro's Taboo, with his parents being half-brother and half-sister. Miss Lanning had decided that it was important to bring in some new and exciting blood and this was embodied in Quillan who became the first American Dane to do just that. The influence that this dog exerted on the breed in the UK was enormous.

It is widely felt by breeders throughout the UK that his son, Fergus, set an unmistakable stamp on his progeny, and this stamp is still clearly recognizable today. Not only was he such a dynamic force as a stud-dog, but his achievements in the ring are also highly acclaimed:

eleven CCs in all, a Group winner and Reserve Best in Show at the City of Birmingham Championship Show.

Mrs J. Cameron made up her first Champion in 1956. This was Ch. Flambonetta of Billil, a daughter of another stud-dog of importance in that era, Ch. Bronx of Blendon out of Flamusine of Billil and bred by Mrs Isaac.

Another first Champion was made up in that same year for Mrs J. Kelly; she was Ch. Surtees of Leesthorphill, a harlequin carrying Wideskies breeding on both sides, Ch. Cloud of Wideskies and Snow of the Wideskies.

In 1958 a fawn male gained his title, Ch. Telluson of Moonsfield, bred by Mr W. Page and owned by Mrs E.M. Harrild, out of Merrie of Merrowlea. The Merrowleas had just started to come into their own and were to play a major part in years to come. I feel a particular affinity with this kennel for it is with their stock that I started to build my own Helmlake lines.

In 1959 Ch. Elch Edler was responsible for no less than three Champions gaining their titles: Miss J.P. Prentis's Ch. Squire of Ridgedaine, Mr J. and Miss L.E. Jackson's Ch. Isobelle of Ashtrees and Miss E. Harrild's Ch. Tellus of Moonsfield.

Another future top-winning kennel starting on the first rungs of the ladder at this time, was the now highly acclaimed Walkmylls. They had started out using Oldmanor and Moonsfield lines to form their breeding programme. In 1965 they made up their first Champion in Ch. Walkmyll Moonyean of Edzell, a fawn bitch sired by Oldmanor Tattoo of Moonsfield out of Aida of Arranton and bred by Mrs L. Edsall. Their next Champion came four years later in their home-bred Ch. Candy of Walkmyll, sired by Ch. Moyalism of Oldmanor out of their first Champion.

In 1976 they imported from the USA Miss Nancy Carroll-Draper's Danelaghs Eurus of Walkmyll whose dam's mother was the litter-sister to Ch. Fergus of Clausentums. It was Eurus who was the cornerstone of the Walkmylls as we know them today. All in all, he sired ten Champions together with several other CC winners. One of these was Ch. Walkmyll Jaeger who won two Best in Shows at general Championship Shows and fourteen CCs in total. Another of Eurus's progeny was Ch. Stranahan Shan of Walkmyll, a winner of six CCs and the dam of two more Champions.

More recently, in the 1980s, the kennel imported from the top Norwegian kennel of Borghild Moen (or Sorenson as she was known before her marriage), Ch. Hotpoints Fortuna of Walkmyll. I had the pleasure of giving this bitch her first CC. This brindle bitch produced Ch. Walkmyll Olivia who herself has won eleven CCs and nine Reserves. Daneagle Elgar of Walkmyll, a descendant of Eurus through Ch. Walkmyll Trestarragon, was the top stud-dog for two years, siring many of the leading Danes in the ring today. Since 1956, twenty-three Champions have carried the Walkmyll prefix.

The first Champion of many for the Merrowleas was made up in 1963, Ch. Squire of Ridgedaine out of Genevieve of Goldendale, bred by Mrs G. Harrison and owned by Mr E.J. Hutton. Another Merrowlea was also to gain his title in this year, Ch. Malloy of Merrowlea, sired by My Choice of Merrowlea out of Marilon of Merrowlea, owned by Miss P. Rossiter and bred by Mrs J. Toye.

In the early 1960s Mrs Eleanor Walshe registered her Sarzec prefix which apparently, according to ancient maps, relates to a township which bordered Babylon and Assyria, the place where it is thought that the Great Dane originated. Three Champions have been bred by the Sarzecs, one of which was Ch. Sarzec Blue Baron who was bred (along with Mrs Jill Coyne) in 1970, sired by Sarzec Blue Saxon out of Kana of Kilcroney. He was the first blue male Champion for over forty years.

It is an interesting fact that only ten blue Champions – five bitches and five dogs – have been bred in England during the last seventy-nine years. The first was in December 1912 and was a bitch, Ch. Ragnhild of Rumgook, while the latest is a dog, Ch. Nightgift Fineas Fogg.

In 1926, the blue Dion of Dicksonia won his third ticket, two in fact awarded by the same judge. (Now the Kennel Club of Great Britain has decreed that a dog must win the three tickets under three separate judges in order to be accorded the title of Champion.) The Send Kennel also produced a blue Champion, Lancelot of Send, in 1930. Then there was Ch. Banshee of Brightonhill who won four CCs in all and dates back to 1949. In the 1950s we had Ch. Margins of Hornsgreen, a blue bitch handled by Dibbie Somerfield; she won eight tickets, gaining her title in 1957. Then, in 1973, a male Champion, Big Sur of Impton, gained his title for Margaret Everton, and the Sarzecs had another blue Champion in Sarzec Blue Stewart who was made up in that year also. Ten years later Ch. Impton Motile won seven tickets in total and was made up in 1983.

In 1962 the Endroma kennel started, one of the most famous from this kennel being Ch. Endroma Morgan's Boy, winner of nine CCs for his owners and breeders Mr and Mrs Russell. They based their bloodlines mainly on Oldmanor and Moonsfield lines who were so predominant and successful, and during the course of their show career have made up four Champions including Ch. The Contender of Dicarl, owned by Di Johnson. In total he won nineteen CCs together with two Working Groups, one of them being at Crufts in 1980.

The Dicarl kennel had a great deal of influence on the breed during the late 1970s and 1980s. The husband and wife team of Di and Carl Johnson decided to base their breeding programmes on Moonsfield and Oldmanor lines after taking their first brood-bitch to an Oldmanor sire who gave them Dicarl Double Up. Taking this generation one step further, she was then mated to Target of Moonsfield who produced two bitches, Dicarl Tarbub and Dicarl Tarbaby.

They decided to take Dicarl Tarbaby to Ch. Simba of Helmlake, and the result of this liaison was Ch. Dicarl The Lioness of Jafrak, while her litter-sister, Dicarl Tarbub went to Ch. Gowerfield Galestorm of Aysdaine who produced another Champion for them, Ch. Dicarl The Heavyweight. The two grandchildren of their foundation brood-bitch were bred to each other and the result of this mating was Ch. The Weightlifter of Dicarl.

In 1965 the Merrowleas were hitting the high spots again, this time with Ch. Merrymonk of Merrowlea who was a son of one of two Merrowlea Champions made up in 1963, the sire being the other Merrowlea-bred dog that had gained his title in 1963, Ch. Malloy of Merrowlea. The combination of Ch. Mallory of Merrowlea and Ch. Goldendale Gay of Merrowlea certainly worked, for they produced four Champions: Ch. Merrymonk of Merrowlea, Ch. Mr Softee of Merrowlea, Ch. Merry Deal of Merrowlea and Ch. Miss Fancy Free of Merrowlea.

In 1965 Mrs E.M. Bacon registered her prefix: Samani. She was at that time interested in German Shepherds and was also actively involved in obedience. She had always liked Great Danes but being so involved with her German Shepherds felt that she probably had neither the time nor the space to do it well.

One day she happened to be driving down the road when she saw a lovely-looking Dane puppy trailing along behind a pram and four children! A couple of weeks later she noticed a sale advertisement in her local paper for a five-month-old Great Dane puppy, and when she went to enquire she was amazed to find out that it was the same puppy she had seen days earlier. The poor puppy appeared to be frightened and decidedly thin; although the owners obviously loved him, it was

Ch. Samani Desert Chief.

purely from ignorance and lack of time that he had fallen into this condition. This turned out to be Godevia of Gowerfield who went on to win two Reserves and become the foundation for this extremely successful kennel. The culmination of their dedication came in the great Ch. Samani Desert Chief who went on to sire ten champions together with several CC- and Reserve-winning children.

Alan, Gwen and Les Herbert are the owners of another well-known kennel, Algwynne; they based their lines first on Oldmanor and then on Dicarl and since 1967 have made up two Champions including the famous Ch. Dicarl The Alliance With Algwynne who was the winner of seventeen CCs, eleven of them with Best of Breed. To add to this impressive record were twelve Reserves. During his show career he was also Reserve in the Working Group, winner of the Champion Stakes and a winner of Pro Dogs. His record is all the more outstanding considering that his owners retired him at four years of age.

Sylvia and Geoff Burton have enjoyed considerable success with their Devarro Kennel. Ch. Devarro Direct Descendant gained his title

Ch. Devarro Direct Descendant. (Photo: Chambers.)

in 1984, and in both 1987 and 1988 he was declared Top Stud-Dog in the breed in the *Dog World*/Pedigree Chum competition. In 1986 and 1988 he was the winner of Top Stud-Dog at the Dane of the Year Show. All in all the stock sired by this dominant sire has totalled thirty CCs between them with six of them gaining their titles to date.

The Burtons decided on the name Devarro when they started to breed Great Danes, which is a variation on a maternal grandmother's name, Devereaux. One of the reasons I am mentioning the various prefixes chosen is that many breeders spend a great deal of time deciding on which name to choose to represent their kennel. This is because it is a name that will represent your dogs and their breeding for, it is to be hoped, many years to come and it needs to be one that you will be happy with.

In 1970, Ch. Kaptain of Kilcroney – a black male – gained his title at three years of age. Also attributed to this kennel and its success was Ch. Talawa of Helmlake of Kilcroney who was a harlequin of great size and substance. He was sired by Ch. Helmlake Chico out of an imported American bitch, Leslie Taura v. Glenbrae.

211

Ch. Miss Freedom of Merrowlea. (Photo: Pearce.)

Mr and Mrs Clement made up their bitch Ch. Gowerfield Candy Caress of Aysdaine in 1970, having bought her from Audrey Shepherd, her breeder; they went on in future years to make up several more Champions. This bitch was a daughter of Ch. Oldmanor Pioneer of Daneii out of Delilah of Aysdaine, bred by Mrs Sheppard, showing how the Oldmanor bloodlines were still having a great influence on the breed.

Also in this year the Reverend and Mrs Davies made up their Ch. Miss Monica of Oldmanor, a very eyecatching and showy bitch who made her mark in the ring.

In 1971 came the first Helmlake Champion, Ch. Miss Freedom of Merrowlea, a daughter of Ch. Merry Deal of Merrowlea out of Miss Carefree of Merrowlea, bred by Capt. and Mrs Hutton. Freedom was bred to Ch. Fergus of Clausentum and the product of this liaison was Ch. Simba of Helmlake, Ch. Malindi of Helmlake and S. Afr. Ch. Voi of Helmlake. In 1971 Ch. Fergus of Clausentum was the proud father of his first two Champions, Ch. Timellie Caspian, who was also the first

212

Champion for Mr and Mrs Harmes-Cooke. In the following year Simba of Helmlake gained his title. Ch. Helmlake Mahe gained her title in 1973; a daughter of Ch. Miss Freedom of Merrowlea, she was sired by the American imported dog Simjeas Hamlet. Her two littermates also gained their titles, Ch. Helmlake Praslin and Ch. Helmlake Curiouse.

In 1968 the Wykendrift kennel came into being under the auspices of Betty Boustead and since that time one Champion and three overseas Champions have been made up. Radiant Roxanna of Nira was the second Dane to be owned by this kennel and, mated to Ch. Gaylaing Astronaut before he gained his title, he produced a promising litter. One of these was to go on to become Ch. Wykendrift Marcellus who was to win five CCs, including Best of Breed at Crufts in 1971, the first time that this lady had ever shown there.

Margaret Everton has been associated with Great Danes since 1968 when she first registered her prefix Impton, basing her breeding programme on Merrowlea stock initially and then combining it with Harmony Hill of the United States and the Airways bloodlines from Sweden. Seven champions have been made up by this clever breeder: two blue, three black, one brindle and one fawn.

Two Danes that have carried the Impton banner proudly were the litter brother and sister combination of Ch. Impton Duralex Bernando and Ch. Impton Duralex Burnita, bred by Mr and Mrs Pettersson. Burnita, a black who was imported from Sweden, was sired by the USA imported dog, Nord. Ch. Harmony Hill Lied of Airways out of Nord. Ch. Chansonette of Doggline and bred by Mr and Mrs Pettersson. She had the distinction of being Margaret's first Champion. Her brother Bernando was made Best in Show at Three Counties in 1973 and was also declared Top Working Dog in the same year. He was the third Impton Champion. Ch. Big Sur of Impton was the second to be made up, and gained his title in 1973. Sired by Ch. Sarzec Blue Baron out of Marpesa of Merrowlea, he was a blue born in 1970 and home-bred.

In 1972, Ch. Dulcie of Haverdane gained her title for her breeders and owners Mr and Mrs Forrest. She was a Dane I had always admired, and it is a great pity that her type is not seen very often in the ring today.

Joyce Wright's Ch. Tarus Major Concession not only had the distinction of gaining his crown, but was also a film star, appearing alongside the distinguished actor Sir Alec Guinness in *Little Lord Fauntleroy* in 1980.

At approximately the same time Mrs J.M. Allan became actively

Int. and Nord. Ch. Impton Duralex Bernando.

involved in the show world with the Dellcourt Great Danes. Her Ch. Dellcourt Auriga was made Best of Breed at Crufts in 1991. The blood-lines go back to Oldmanor- and Moonsfield-based stock.

The Dorneywood kennel was first started in 1972 by Mr and Mrs Parish, basing their breeding on Oldmanor and Clausentum lines. Their type is easily recognized and has proved a dominant force in the show ring with eleven UK Champions made up over the years. Associated with the Dorneywood kennel is Anne Adamson through Ch. Dorneywood Sebastian; her other Champion, Ch. Drumview Heir Apparent, goes back to strong Dorneywood lines.

Sue Yule (now Pollock) has made up two Champions over the years, Ch. Bencleves Bobcat and Ch. Buster of Bencleves. The kennel name was chosen because of the kennel's close proximity to the house 'Cleves Cross', where, inscribed into the stone wall of the yard, was the date 1200, when the last boar in England met its end at the hands of one Roger De Ferry. Given the Great Dane's connection with the boarhound, it was decided to link the 'Cleves' with the name 'Ben', Ben being the name of her first Dane.

Ch. Eastlight Second Edition became a Champion in 1990 although the kennel of Steve and Pat Townend had been connected with Great Danes since 1974. The Eastlight kennel has been founded on mainly Dicarl bloodlines which go back to the Moonsfield and Oldmanor stock via Ch. Simba of Helmlake and then Ch. Fergus of Clausentum.

In 1978 Nigel Marriner registered his prefix Marridane and – in partnership with Elaine Harrison – has made up two Champions. Their lines have been based on Helmlake, Oldmanor and Walkmyll. Their Ch. Helmlake Quo Vadis of Marridane is probably the one who brought them to the fore, winning ten CCs, Reserve in the Working Group at Windsor, twice Best in Show at Open Show level and winner of the East of England section of the Pedigree Chum Champion Stakes. Their second Champion, Batworth Obsession at Marridane, began her glittering career in 1990, gaining her first CC at Bath at just fourteen months old. She won her crown at Crufts in 1991, judged Best Dane Bitch by Olive Davies (Oldmanor). When 'Sessy' tragically died at the age of only three and a half years in the summer of 1992, she was the fifth top winning Great Dane of all time with twenty-three CCs and four Reserve CCs. She was sired by Imperial Emperor of Helmlake and was half-sister to the youngest Helmlake Champion, Ch. Helmlake Take My Fashion, who won her first CC at nineteen months old.

Anne Hartley and Sally Chadwick are renowned for their Picanbil Great Danes which were originally registered in 1978. Their love of dogs generated from their father who was a breeder of Greyhounds. Sallust Marquisite was the first Dane owned by them, affectionately known as Aunty Margot. They have won multiple CCs with such dogs as Ch. Picanbil Pericles, having been guided by Ann Foxwell and basing their lines on Oldmanor and Airways. Ch. Samani Desert Chief was the sire of both their Champions.

Anne Foxwell registered the Auldmoor prefix in 1972 and since then has made up seven English Champions and two overseas. Her lines have been based on Oldmanor and Airways as she was able to acquire Oldmanor Manthem from the Reverend and Mrs Davies, who gained her title carrying the Auldmoor name as well.

Also behind her breeding programme come the American lines of Honeylanes and Rojons and Harmony Hill, the latter being behind the Airways prefix. Ch. Arianne of Auldmoor figures highly in the Auldmoor kennel for she was BIS at the Dane of The Year Show and Reserve BIS at the Working Breeds in 1984, as well as a winner of the Midland Counties Pedigree Petfoods Champion Stakes.

The desire to import, generally from the German stock, has not diminished over the years and it is from imported stock that Sylvia

MacGowan has based her own Asoud Great Danes. She brought into the UK Enrico Vom Drawehner Wald of Asoud and Elyshia Vom Aquator of Asoud who, as both had been cropped in their native land, were unable to to be shown here.

Mr and Mrs Bousfield registered their kennel name in 1980 following Sherain, Walkmyll, Impton and Oldmanor lines initially and more recently adding Daneagle and Samani. In this time they have made up five Champions including Ch. Yacanto I'm Mandy who also had the honour of being made Best Puppy at the Dane of the Year Show in 1988.

Rick and Jan Day made up Ch. Janriche He's Daring and credit most of their success to the Dicarl lines. He's Daring has to date won five CCs, was Dane of the Year in 1990 and was the leading male in the SWGDC 'Superleague' of the same year.

Shaun MacAlpine will be remembered with great affection in and out of the breed. He enjoyed a lifetime's love of the breed which was nurtured by his parents who were regular participants at the shows. Their stand 'Cessmac', was famed throughout the land for having some beautiful, and rare models of various breeds.

Shaun will probably best be remembered for his partnership with his beloved Ellie, Ch. Dicarl Tendellie. It was a pleasure to see this part-nership as a team in the ring, both handler and exhibit in tune with each other. Tendellie won multiple CCs and her success was extended to the Working Group at Crufts, a year after her father, Ch. The Contender of Dicarl, merited the same award. However, Ellie was deprived of her devoted handler when at only twenty-one years of age Shaun was killed in a motorway crash. The sight of Ellie in the church on the day of Shaun's funeral reduced many a strong person to tears as she bade her own farewell to her friend and master.

It is almost impossible to record every person or breeder who has contributed towards the breed; some dedicate their lives to helping to enhance the breed, some stay in the breed for a short time only. All the time there are new breeders and fanciers taking up the challenge. One of these is Laurence Evans: with his kennel registered in 1986 he has already made up one Champion. There are also Lesley and Adam Chappell with their Champion Walkmyll Flare of Selmalda, Pat and Ann Jacobs, Jim and Lynne Donnelly, and Anne Asquith who has been in the breed for nearly ten years and although she has not made up a Champion yet, she says she is still trying.

I first met Janice and Peter King, prefix Eppwood, along with their daughter Samantha in 1985 when they purchased a brindle bitch, Octavia of Helmlake. The sole idea at that time was to have a loving

Ch. Dicarl Tendellie.

pet but fate decreed otherwise. Octavia was bred by Mrs C. Vaughan, sired by Ch. and Sp. Ch. Cid Campeador de los Madronales of Helmlake, and her dam was Hamfelde Shoot That Tiger. Octavia turned into such a beauty that the show world beckoned. The King family made her into a Champion and later mated her to their second Dane, Helmlake Timber. The progeny of these two fine Danes are now showing with great success.

Another up-and-coming breeder is Corinna Hamer, prefix Corindane, who has based her breeding on Wharflake and Helmlake lines. Totally dedicated to the breed, she will be a force to be reckoned with in the future.

Linda Austen with her Grovemandy Danes has bred two bitches with tickets, and another with six Reserves. Susan Cottrell and her black and blue Berevale Great Danes have also contributed towards the breed. Ch. Metrelle Academus was made up by Marion and Charles Hipkin, Ch. Danemoor the Persian Boy by Phil and Olivia Bates, and Ch. Dicarl Who's Free by Dr and Mrs Kumar.

Tony and Julie Schanning Ling have been breeding and showing Danes for almost twenty years. They have had success with their

Ch. Helmlake Take My Fashion.

brindle bitch Gemflora Ice Dance at Galomax, having based their breeding on Gemflora and Nightsgift lines.

Mrs Pam Price is one of our newer exhibitors, registering her prefix in 1988, who has been enjoying great success with Endroma Leopold, bred by Rae and Peter Russell and sired by Helmlake Brioche. I should mention Helen and Tom Hankins as well, with their Woodelrond Centurion and Woodelrond Canderelle, and Lisa Fletcher with Zebatique Zultar who, plus other notable wins, has a Reserve.

Averill Thorndyke began her career in 1972 with her fawn bitch Timellie Cinora. Continuing the lines of Timellie and Gracelove, she had considerable success. In 1974 the lines of Gaymiles and Helmlake took her into the world of harlequins. She mated Gaymiles Belinda with Ch. Helmlake Implicable, and produced her Int. Ch. French Fashion of Helmlake.

All these people, amongst others throughout the Great Dane's history, have devoted themselves to this magnificent breed and gained a terrific amount of enjoyment. It is important, though, to put back into the breed the pleasure that you receive, and never to tamper with the good that has been achieved. The fate of the breed lies in the hands of the breeders and the judges, and between them they create future Champions. They controlled the past and we are responsible for the present and the future. Remember that if you decide to join the dedicated ranks, it is up to you to try to help improve the breed and to do your best for it.

Appendix

Useful Addresses

The Kennel Club
1/4 Clarges Street
Piccadilly
London
Tel: 071 493 6651

The Great Dane Club of
    America
442 Country View Lane
Garland
Texas 75043
USA

East of England Great Dane
    Club
Mrs H. Pearce
White House Farm Kennels
Stutton Lane
Stutton
Ipswich
Suffolk IP9 2SX
Tel: 0473 328295

Great Dane Breeders
    Association
Mrs M. Stevens
Highfield
Longfield Avenue
New Barn
Nr Dartford
Kent DA3 7LA
Tel: 04747 3470

Great Dane Club
Mrs F. C. Lewis
Lodge Farm
Bridgtown
Cannock
Staffordshire WS11 3LT
Tel: 0922 413354

Great Dane Club of South Wales
Mrs M. Jeffries
Riverside Bungalow
Old Furnace Road
Trecenydd
Caerphilly
Mid Glamorgan CF8 2RP
Tel: 0222 861903

Midland and West of England
    Great Dane Club
Mrs S. M. Burton
167 Mansfield Road
Papplewick
Nottinghamshire NG15 8FL
Tel: 0602 632743

Northern Great Dane Club
Mr J. Taylor
Westleigh
35 Chamber Road
Shaw
Greater Manchester OL2 7AR
Tel: 0706 845755

Pennine Great Dane Club
Mrs S. Yule
The Rectory
Thorndale Road
Thorney Close
Sunderland SR3 4JT
Tel: 091 528 6613

Scottish Great Dane Club
Mrs J. Christie
The Gabel
Bellevue Avenue
Kirkintilloch
Glasgow
Strathclyde G66 1AT
Tel: 041 776 3665/4390

South Western Great Dane Club
Mr W. A. Spurin
The Copse
Huish Champflower
Nr Wiveliscombe
Taunton
Somerset TA4 2HG
Tel: 0984 24003

Further Reading

Alderton, D., *The Dog Manual*, Popular Dogs.

Brown, Curtis M., *Dog Locomotion and Gait Analysis*, Hoflyn Publishing Ltd.

de Bairacli Levy, J., *Complete Herbal Book of the Dog*, Faber & Faber.

Carrol-Draper, Nancy, *The Great Dane: Dogdom's Apollo*, Howell Book House Inc.

Elliott, R.P., *Dogsteps Illustrated; Gait at a Glance*, Howell Book House Inc.

Harmer, Hilary, *Dogs and How to Breed Them*, John Gifford Ltd.

Hart, Ernest, *This is the Great Dane*, T. F. H. Publications.

Heal, R., *He Whacked the Bloody Lot – Bill Siggers*, Andrew Brace.

Holst, P., *Canine Reproduction: A Breeder's Guide*, Alpine.

Lanning, Jean, *Great Danes*, Popular Dogs.

Little, C. C., *Inheritance of Coat Colour in Dogs*, Howell Book House Inc.

McDonald, Bruce, *All About the Great Dane*, Pelham Books Ltd.

McDowell Lyon, *The Dog in Action*, Howell Book House Inc.

Messent, Peter, *Understanding Your Dog*, MacDonald and Co. Ltd.

Mindell, Earl, *The Vitamin Bible*, Arlington Books (1982).

Morris, Desmond, *Dogwatching*, Jonathan Cape.

Robinson, Roy, *Robinson's Genetics for Dog Breeders*, Pergamon Press.

Sandys-Winsch, Godfrey, *Your Dog and the Law*, Shaw & Sons.

Willis, Dr Malcolm B., *Genetics of the Dog*, H. F. and G. Witherby Ltd.

Index